PEACE & JOY WITHIN YOU

10 Lessons In

Spiritual Freedom

(Going Beyond Religion)

Touching The Source of

Enlightenment

Ramas Dev

ISBN-13: 978-0692518014

ISBN-10: 0692518010

Perspective Publishing

PerspectivePublishing@mail.com

FORETHOUGHT

Pronouns like "he," "she," or "it" is only applicable in the realm of form. Form is an attribute of and to the mind. The spiritual realm is One, and as such there is no separation.

God is never threatened, least by a mere human or his action, speech, or thought. Even a thought in the mind is not his.

God does not need a human to defend Him, Her, or It. For example, if someone burns a religious book, that shows darkness in the person burning the book. If people are angered by someone burning a religious book or drawing a caricature of a religious figure then both parties are reacting through the carnal mind, and as such both add fuel to the fire. If one's God needs human defense then that person needs to seek another God, for the God who needs human protection is not the **Almighty God**.

God is not necessarily pleased by ten thousand praises, nor angered by a curse. God who reacts according to the mind is not God. It may be a man or an angel proclaiming as God, beware.

God will not tell us to kill other people who do not practice what we believe in, or who do not look like us in terms of race, culture, language, ethnicity, or nationality.

Apart from God there is nothing because God Is (everything), and nothing (no-thing) has no existence.

Spiritual knowledge is rather selective in a sense that unless we are ready for it, we are not able to realize it even though we may be reading it.

Good or bad is an interpretation of the mind.

God is "no mind" because God is beyond the mind. Yet, a thought that comes to the mind is of God.

The carnal mind is always defensive and propped up. With no ego to support the mind is free, and the Self is freely revealed.

To transcend the encapsulating concepts and notions of the mind as a human unravels the false self of the mind representation (the ego) and *realizes* what Is (behind the illusion) should be the main objective of our life. For that is the way to our freedom from this world of suffering, the curse of being born in this fallen world, this samsara.

So why were we born?

Though on a broader scale, realization of one's true Self is the answer, yet we should not discount the positive aspect of doing good. Good deeds add heavenly treasure or good Karma to our soul, and good karma then serves as a fuel towards our spiritual destination (realization of our true Self).

The Kingdom Of God

The kingdom of God is all encompassing, which is within and without.

The kingdom of God is here and now.

The kingdom of God is becoming nothing to the world.

The kingdom of God is the path of self-sacrifice.

The kingdom of God is becoming one in (with) the Spirit of God, which is the Self-realization, or being aware of the essence of God within us.

The kingdom of God does not come by our desire or pressure; it happens when we become ready, and it happens unexpectedly.

The kingdom of God is like a free flowing river. A leaf that falls on water flows with/by the current of the water.

The kingdom of God is like a ripple on a still pond which starts in the middle (heart) of the pond and spreads all over.

The kingdom of God is like when a man lost all he had and then he realized that he had nothing else to lose, who then rejoiced and went home in peace.

The kingdom of God is like walking in a straight path and after walking for awhile coming to the place where one had begun to walk, whereupon the man rejoiced and rested.

If we know what is within us then we have known what is beyond the world, but if we know what is before us and not what is within then we are, indeed, ignorant.

The greatest tragedy in the world is the sense of separation from the rest. In it lies all the wars, all selfish hoardings, callousness, and the human misery.
The mind separates, but the Spirit is One. We are all connected in the Spirit. We are like colorful petals in a beautiful flower.

"कून मन्दिरमा जान्छौ यात्री?"

"Which Temple Will You Go, O Seeker?"

Written by Late Nepali Poet *Laxmi Prashad Devkota*
Translated from Nepali by Ramas Dev

*Which temple will you go, O seeker? Which temple will
you seek?*
*What substance will you offer to God? How will you carry
it to heaven with you?*

*Made with the beautiful pillars of bone, with the outer
wall of flesh.*
*Adorned with the golden roof of head, eyes as windows
to the world.*
*Ever flowing rivers that make up the veins, you are the
real temple, O seeker!*

Which temple will you go, O seeker?

A lonely seeker on the road, yet God walks with him.
Blesses God the ones who work hard,
with a touch of miracle on those who serve others.

Which temple will you go, O seeker? Which temple will
you seek?
What substance will you offer to God? How will you carry
it to heaven with you?

Return, O seeker, rather wash other's feet,
cover their open wounds, salve their affliction.
Bring joy on someone's face, for God rejoices with such.
Which temple will you go, O seeker?

God sings in the chirping of birds by the roadside.
God calls you through the agony and pain of others.
Yet you won't see God with these eyes, nor hear God
with these ears!

Which temple will you go, O seeker? Which temple will
you seek?
What substance will you offer to God? How will you carry
it to heaven with you?

CON **TEN** TS

INTRODUCTION

This book is an outcome of going through the fiery furnace of life, through dealing with the unexpected trials and tribulations in life which have shaped me and helped me to identity myself, through facing the struggles, and attempts in conquering the fears which dominated much of the life. It is the downs in life which help us rise above and search beyond ourselves. When life is too comfortable, the mind does not find much incentive to think beyond itself or the world.

I write this book with a hope that it will help others to think beyond the conventional religious beliefs or even unbelief. I urge you to have an open mind while reading this book. Belief system is very resistive to change, and people tend to react bitterly, especially if their religious belief is challenged. Having said that, I respect whatever your belief may be, and yet I implore you to push any barrier you encounter as you practice and explore in your religious belief. *Always remember that the Spirit of God sets us free from all bondage, and the Almighty God can never be threatened*. When we acknowledge this truth, we find the comic futility that is going on in the world in the name of religion where people use violence to justify their religious ideologies.

We have this treasure hidden within us, which so many of us fail to realize. Whether we believe in God or accept God in our own unique way, we can have our personal relationship with God to channel the strength, love, joy, and peace in the Spirit. Even if we say that we do not believe in God, yet that does not exclude us from reaching deep within ourselves to feel that "something" which enables us to overcome painful circumstances we face in life. As we reach closer to that "something," our perspective about life changes, and we change. Just because people say that they are an atheist does not null or void what is! When a child closes its eyes, will the world go dark? Sure the child may think otherwise, but the reality should not be discounted.

I acknowledge that the thoughts that come into the mind are not exclusive to mine. There is no mine and yours in the Consciousness that encompasses everything. Everything is, and there is nothing new under the sun. However, as someone rightly said, "Why invent a wheel?" It is much easier to walk in the path already paved by someone before us. That does not preclude us from seeking further or reaching new heights. Life, as we know it here on the earth, is finite or rather very short to go on like "wine tasting" when it comes to what to base our belief or faith on. Having said that, we should not become 'religious' or hardheaded in one thing we find ourselves in, and become fixed or resist in exploring further. Even though the Spirit knows everything yet we are in the flesh, and as a carnal man we are governed by the mind. However, we need to transcend the carnal mind to realize the oneness with the Spirit, which is the perfection of our soul.

This book is not meant to explain about religions or God, although it deals with the said topics. Infinite God is beyond the comprehension through the finite mind. However, it is my understanding that life becomes much easier if we trust God, and entrust our burden onto God. It is also the process of our spiritual maturity, which is like climbing a mountain wherein we see through new perspective as we climb higher. We do not necessarily need to subscribe to any particular belief system in order to be spiritual. What is outside points to what is within us. The Spirit is the source of our strength, and our true identity.

The Spirit of God is within us.

If your concept of God is limited to an old man with white hair and beard in a long white robe walking in the clouds, or an idol or a statue, then your views about God will be challenged as you read this book. While at the same time, that does not mean that your views or concepts are necessarily wrong. Please have an open mind while reading this book, as it is impossible to finitely define God, nor put the infinite God in a box of mental abstraction. When we say, "I know God," then we are confronted with the ambiguity about God. It is rather safe to use vague terms like omnipotent, omnipresent, omniscient, love, etc. to attribute God.

The title of this book says, **"Ten Lessons In Spiritual Freedom**," and each chapter is like a spoke on a wheel which points to the hub, the Spirit of God within us. Any act of kindness, forgiveness, or surrender to God takes us closer to the heart of our being. The chapters in this book may seem to overlap by the name of their title, however as you read through the chapters you will find new spiritual flowers in them. However, this book is not a ten steps program. Each chapter can be read individually without first reading the preceding chapters. Read it however way it appeals to you. Keep walking, and eventually you will reach your destination.

Each chapter covers topics that help to overcome the limitation of the carnal mind. The book is not organized in any special order. However, each chapter uses a diamond symbol (◊) to separate topics. This is done to help a reader with the necessary breaks. Feel free to pause and contemplate, or practice along at each break.

This book tries to push religious boundaries, even though religious verses are used. One has to go beyond concepts or notions to realize truth. The mind works in concepts and notions, while the Spirit is just beyond the mind. Although it may seem conflicting, different concepts can point to the same thing. Hence it is wise not to hold onto a concept. The spiritual realm is, indeed, paradoxical. Take an example used in this book as a tool to understand the meaning of a truth. A tool is not an end in itself, but rather is like a ladder to help us climb up, and when we have climbed up we do not hang on to the ladder. The water footprints left by a duck's feet out of a pond disappear soon after it walks away.

Among the other topics in this book, you will read that you are not defined by your circumstances, no matter how unpleasant or dire they may seem or be. You have the power and the authority to define your life. Many of the topics that are mentioned in this book may seem obvious to you. This is because of the spiritual nature of the book. The Spirit knows all, and deep within you, in your heart, is the Spirit of God. Yet obvious things in life are often overlooked. Few topics in this book may seem repetitive, and in a sense they are. However, they are presented from different perspectives in order to make them more comprehensive and *obvious*. Things need to make sense for the mind to attach itself to.

Chapter three makes a segue by delving in the topic about God, the Spirit, and Consciousness through technical perspective. Such attempt is not meant to explain God, who is unexplainable, but rather to make spiritual concepts more clear. Often it is easier to understand a topic if it relates to what we are already familiar with.

Religious verses are quoted where appropriate in this book. Please do not be stuck or overtly concerned if you have not read the Bible, the Dhammapada, or other religious books referenced in this book, or if it seems that the references are presented from a different perspective. Try to take wisdom behind the words. *Be like a merchant who travels far and wide seeking fine pearls.* God is beyond a religion. A religion can guide us in our journey, but it can also be a hindrance in our Self-realization. So, I urge you to have an open mind while reading this book. Do not let religiosity be an impediment to you.

When confronted with a concept which may seem conflicting to your rooted belief, try to look from a different angle. Be assured that truth is beyond a concept and can never be threatened. Jesus spoke in parables which can be interpreted in many ways, and who can say that their interpretation is the only correct one? Thus, a parable can give us a personal interpretation, and yet, at the same time, be ambiguous to others. Short illustrations are used throughout this book to help understand a concept or clarify a thought. Illustrations are always helpful in remembering what we have read because the mind likes to "picture" things. If a certain example does not feel appropriate, try to think from a different perspective. God does not necessarily speak to us the same word even if it were for the same matter.

Do not feel in any way pressured while reading this book. Take your time, and go with your pace. Just make sure that you are moving, and not stuck at one place. It is easy for the mind to lose interest in a new endeavor and give up. It is so effortless to let the world move us, after all much of the world is under the dominion of the carnal mind. It is only through the grace of God that we are spiritually born. Life is not a race or a competition. Simply reading any spiritual book will only amuse the mind and will probably give some topics of conversation with friends, but the actual power or transformation comes from the application of knowledge. Thus, knowledge is powerful, but it is not power.

If we are meant to benefit from a certain knowledge, we will find the knowledge any way. Time is not a constraint in the spiritual realm. It is my personal experience that if we were not ready to read a certain book then we would not read it, even if we were handed the book. It is important to let the Spirit of God move us. We do good when we walk in love. When we do good, we heap heavenly treasure which then affects our life positively. Yet even the will to do good happens through the will of God. That is why it is very important to be humble and patient so that we are able to recognize the subtle prompts that are given to us in the Spirit. When we walk according to the dictates of the flesh, either we are distracted and thus not able to hear the voice of God, or we are not willing to heed the loud and clear voice of God. Regardless, we fall when we walk in the flesh.

This book is written in rather informal manner, much like I'm talking to someone, to you. Spiritual lessons are subjective, and I feel that this way of trying to reach or show something is more effective than merely writing about the meaning of different spiritual terms. I hope that this book will give you new insight, inspire you to seek beyond what is "normal," open up new possibilities in your life in terms of dealing with your struggles in life, and nudge you to seek peace and joy in life. Spiritual fruit like love, peace, or joy is always free and always available. It is my hope that this book will help you in some way, no matter how small it may be; I will consider it a success.

God Bless All

(Namasté – I bow before the Divine in you.)

To God who desires the first fruit off of us.
To my parents, Maya and Rameshwor, and family who
are a big part of me, and who love me unconditionally.

"The kingdom of God is within you"

- Luke 17:21

ACKNOWLEDGMENTS

To the Holy Spirit of God who is and whose voice speaks through us all.

I am grateful to everyone whom my path crossed, and in whom I have found love; it is indeed encouraging.

Daniel, my spiritual brother, you are an encouragement in walking in love.

I'd like to thank Eckhart Tolle for his book "The Power Of NOW," and Dr. David R. Hawkins for his book "Transcending The Levels Of Consciousness." They were an inspiration.

Special thanks to Mr. Kenneth McDonald who advised me with technical information in the preparation of this book.

1 ACCEPT LIFE NO MATTER WHAT

**Change is what is constant in this Universe.
If you are going through a difficult situation in life,
have patience because that too shall pass.**

We live in the world where we are constantly bombarded by views and opinions about pretty much anything; from the name for our unborn children to what will happen after our physical death. One thing that all of these make obvious is that life on this earth is imperfect according to our expectations, because expectations are limitless while their fulfillment is limited or scarce. This brings about unnecessary dissatisfaction, conflicts, frustrations, even depression and other ills in our life. However, when we accept life as it is and no matter what then that helps us ease or remove the resistance that we have in the mind from our wrongful expectations of life.

It is like removing an imaginary wall which we have built all of our life which has shrouded our perspective and caused us much suffering.

When we accept this malady of life, this constant tug-of-war of our endless expectations, desires, and unending cravings on the one hand, and the reality of this imperfect and limited world on the other hand, then we open a door for peace and joy in our life. Now, for most of us, this seems so obvious and even downright silly when someone says to us, "Deny what is not, and accept what is real." However, oftentimes we have to ask ourselves if we are falling into the same pitfall of grasping vanity over and over again. *Simple things in life are often ignored or overlooked.* We need to revise our priorities in life to the point where we are freed from the derivation of our sense of happiness from ephemeral material things or other people to something lasting and eternal which is available in the Spirit of God.

◊

Acknowledging the reality that joy is found within us and not outside is like finding the true north in the compass of our life. Often, people are inclined to appreciate their life after they have gone through life changing events like major sickness, accident, incarceration, etc. When people hit their rock bottom, and they accept the reality as an undeniable part of their life, granted that it is never easy, then they find new appreciation for life. The world and its ways are the hindrance to our soul in realizing peace and joy in the Spirit.

When we accept the shortcomings in the flesh and this fallen world then we are able to experience the sense of serenity. We feel the negative forces that have kept us under their control, because of our tendency to defend the ego, now loosening their grip on us. When we acknowledge a reality, there is no need to guard an unreality, which then frees us from the fear of both the reality and the unreality. Reality, no matter how uncomfortable, is better than living in a fantasy world. Life is in the living, being alive in this very moment. Everything in this world changes, and even our unpleasant circumstance changes into something different and better. *Accepting our reality is like shining the light over the darkness of unreality.*

◊

Life is like a garland of moments; some moments are pleasant while others are painful. It is the tendency of the mind to revel and enjoy easy times, but drag through the difficult times. Who can say that they are immune to life's tumultuous moments? When we look back in our life we see both types of circumstances, good and bad, or pleasant and sorrowful. However, when we are going through difficult times, it seems all unfair to us as though the world has turned its back on us to the point that it appears like we are the only one enduring the blunt of the misfortune. Many people who commit suicide cannot accept their life as it is. They are overwhelmed by the enormity of their life situation. Constant thinking about our problems is worrying, which only fuels the vicious cycle of more negative thoughts spiraling into the mind, getting bigger and confounding us. Thus, by worrying, the mind makes a mountain out of a mole.

We need to shift our perspective from negative to positive when going through a difficult situation in life so that we are able to cope in such circumstances. The issue is the same, but with the change of our viewpoint we are able to overcome difficulties in life. Usually when we have passed through a difficult phase in life, we realize that it was not as insurmountable as we thought it was. However, when life becomes "normal" or easy again, we have the tendency to forget about our struggles.

Our circumstances, no matter how difficult, will change. We need to have patience and wait. Yet, we do not wait while we live, we live while we wait. Life does not let us hold on to the fond moments forever, nor does it let us put off those prickly ones. When life seems overwhelming, internalize this wisdom that life goes on no matter what. The sun does not stop rising for us, nor the moon stops rotating for us. Try to be unmoved by the circumstances in life, realizing that you have your life, and the circumstances are only temporary.

It is rather a cliché to hear that life is full of ups and downs, yet it is the truth we need to acknowledge. If we let ourselves be swung like a pendulum by the circumstances in life then we are essentially giving up our joy, peace, and freedom. Never think that you will not be able to get up when you fall down, no matter how hard or low you fall. If you take courage to move on, mountains in your life will move for you because those mountains in life are also subjected to the law of constant change.

Do not be overtly happy during the sunny days of life, nor be overtly sorrowful during the rainy days of life. Be life a pilgrim who passes through a land without stopping for too long or investing too much of himself at one place. Be like a leaf that falls on a river flowing by the virtue of the current of the water. *Joy comes from within when we realize that there is nothing to lose and that we are complete and perfect in the Spirit.* The mind cannot realize this because it dwells in the state of constant scarcity. As we overcome desires and cravings of the flesh, we find lasting happiness in our being.

◊

Accepting life as it is no matter what does not mean that we become passive in inaction and we let the world bulldoze us and push us to the landfills of life. Rather it is like laying a solid foundation before building a house. Without first being willing to accept our current circumstance, our plans and actions will be based on our wish, desire, or fantasy. This will more than likely lead us further into the mire of dissatisfaction with our projection on the circumstance askew. N*o matter how* *excruciating our circumstance may seem, we have the final say on whether we overcome the circumstance, or we let the circumstance overcome us.* Pessimism combined with inaction leads to our circumstance overcoming us, whereas accepting our reality with positive outlook on life paves the way for constructive actions. When we acknowledge a truth, we are set free from dwelling in the past. It is like putting down a huge burden from our back, and being able to run freely.

Meditation On Letting Go

Spend some time regularly by yourself without any distraction. Like a snake that sheds its dead skin behind, let go of all of your burdens.

Focus on your breath as you breathe calmly and deeply.

Allow what is bubbling beneath in the mind to surface.

Pray silently if you are led to.

Channel the strength in the Spirit by focusing on the issue at hand. Let the power of the Spirit empower you. Do not actively think about an issue. Be an audience to the thoughts as they come to the mind. Let thoughts come and go, like pictures on a movie screen, with you being actively grounded in the present moment with your breath as your prop.

Do not try to grasp or dwell on any thought. No

judging either.

Be still, and let the Spirit set you free as the mind is conditioned so that the issue losses its strength to you.

It is a good practice to regularly sync with the Spirit. The mind is otherwise very active and even downright shameless in taking back its control over us. Do not antagonize the mind, either. Accept what is. In other words, do not deny your present reality. Know that difficult situations are a part of life, but they do not define you. Try to be comfortable with yourself, and with the silence of being alone. Without the constant noise, the mind is available and attentive. Take a personal survey of your daily activities, and prioritize them. Activities like watching TV, using excessive internet, shopping, social gossips, etc. need to be replaced by activities like reading, prayer, meditation, fellowship with spiritually minded circle, charity, etc. which engender spiritual maturity in us.

◊

If we are not in a good situation in life and something bad is about to happen then we should not lose our hope in life. Without hope we tend to take detrimental steps in life which further jeopardize the already unpleasant situation, whereupon we end up regretting for the very things we ruined willy-nilly. The mind has the easy tendency to give up under pressure. Thoughts like "My good is never enough, what's the point?" or "Well, it's going to happen anyway, so might as well do this thing" is a common voice of the mind. The ego is destructive to the point that it will sacrifice the self than accept that it is wrong. We can have some breather in a difficult situation if we try to find a positive aspect in it, no matter how small. However, the carnal mind will readily focus on negativity because it is filled with uncertainties with its limited knowledge. Where there are uncertainties, fear is not lacking. So we need to make an active effort in goading the mind along the path which is well lit with the spiritual lamp.

◊

Uncertainties and unknowns can cause much fear and even pain in our life. Even though they are not real as they have not been manifested or happened by their virtue of being uncertain or unknown, yet in the mind they are very real and wreck much havoc. Just think about when you were in school and the feeling you may had before an exam, or before your job interview. Did you feel nervous despite your self-confidence? Most people feel the tension even if they are well prepared.

When we are confronted with something that "might" happen, we can ask ourselves, *"So what?"* to the circumstance.

Lost your job?

"So what?" Have you never lost a job or known

someone who has lost a job?

Rejected by someone?

"*So what?*" Have you never received "no" for an answer, or known someone who has been ditched and yet they are happy with someone else now?

Facing an illness?

"*So what?*" Have you never fallen sick? Are you the only one to suffer?

It may seem like everything is against us when we are going through such trying times. Yet we can overcome any circumstance, and we have so far. *Do not have "all or nothing" attitude in life*. You may or may not be able to get back to the same height you were before in terms of job position, wealth, or health, but life goes on. *Regardless of everything that is wrong in life, experiencing life is a blessing in itself*. We just need to reorient ourselves to appreciate what is right in life. In fact what is simple in life is often precious and important. For example, having a loving family is a blessing.

◊

From Worrier To Spiritual Warrior

Worrying never does us any good. Even if a doctor has said that a person has only a short while to live, what does worrying benefit anything to the person? It will only make the person's remaining days miserable, including everyone around. Rather, the person can accept the painful reality by making peace with himself or herself, which then fuels humility, love, and appreciation for life and everything. The person will be like a beautiful flower with sweet smelling fragrance emanating despite the thorns of illness.

Even the prospect of physical death need not keep us away from enjoying our life. If we need an inspiration to appreciate our life fully because we have been fortunate so far by not having to face life's excruciating phases then we can volunteer our time in helping others who are terminally ill. In doing so gives us an opportunity to learn the value of each moment of our own life with new zeal. Each smile, each encouraging word, each action inspired by love, each prayer with empathy, and each compassionate thought emanates new passion for life in us.

◊

Life is in the living and living freely without the fetter of remorse from our past. There is a difference between being regretful and dragging the regrets along with us. Being sorry is a sign of humility and opens the door for reconciliation, harmony, peace, and freedom, while keeping the burden of regret within ourselves obstructs the free flow of life energy in us. When we make a mistake, we need to be open and willing to acknowledge that we are indeed sorry. This helps us by not keeping us in the darkness of fear, guilt, shame, and pride where we beat ourselves down for a mistake. We all make mistakes, big and small. Let your past mistakes be lessons for you, like pictures in your yearbook which you browse rarely and then move on with your life. *Do not let the past be a stumbling block for your present life, make peace with yourself and let the past be a stepping stone for your future.*

The best "Time Machine" a man has is the present moment. This moment which is flowing so smoothly and otherwise unnoticeable if we do not take "time" and be mindfully planted in this very moment like a tree rooted firmly on a bank of a river (as pictured in **Psalm 1**). If our action has caused others hurt or harm then we can use this present moment to take a constructive action and reconcile with them. We cannot go back in time and correct our wrong in the past, but we can do what is needed in the present to make it right for us and others, mend relationships, and bring peace in us and others. Do not let pride be a hindrance for your soul. Pride is not our friend, but an enemy in disguise. Pride is like a makeup that an actor wears to look beautiful which eventually comes off. Humbleness is the inner beauty that is hard to go unnoticed but often ignored in the world. Humility is our true essence, and it brings peace and joy within and without.

◊

Take time to look at things around you in nature; look at the ants scurrying around while carrying bits and pieces of leaves. Look at the flowers that open up to sunrise. Look at the birds flying in the sky completely free; they migrate to a distant land without worrying about what will happen to the place they leave behind. Everything in the nature is just happening, and everything continues to happen just perfectly until this "I" or the ego comes into play. We start to imagine things that "could" or "might" happen and try to alter the normal course of events. Ants do not worry, flowers do not lose their petals over a possible drought, nor do birds lose their sleep over their past or future. Even a grasshopper that loses its limb to its predator does not just sit there worrying about what has happened to it, nor drag along its severed limb, saying "Poor me!" The grasshopper moves on swiftly leaving the dead (limb) behind, and saves its life from its predator. We, too, need to move on with our life without dragging our dead past before the past chokes life out of the present or before death overshadows our life.

"Let the dead bury their dead."

We need to do what we can, and leave everything else to God. What can we do otherwise? God is more than able to take care of everyone and everything in the creation. To think that we, as the ego, know more than God, who is eternal and all knowing, is a fallacy. By ourselves, we are reduced to nothing.

"All flesh is grass, and all its loveliness is like the flower

of the field. The grass withers, the flower fades, because the breath of the Lord blows on it; surely the people are like grass. The grass withers, the flower fades, but (the word of our) God stands forever ."

- Isaiah 40:6- 8

◊

You are not defined by what others think you are, nor what others say about you. When you know who you really are then you are free from the need to be according to other's expectations, even yours also. *There is really no need to prove anything to anyone.*

"So who are you? "

Do you identify with what you see on a mirror?

Do you identify with your job? How much money you make, or your social status?

Do you identify with your political affiliation?

How about your religious belief?

To know who we are, we need to transcend the form and pry into the essence of our being.

"Again, the kingdom of heaven is like treasure hidden in a field, which a man found and hid; and for joy over it he goes and sells all that he has and buys that field ."

- Matthew 13:44

Everything the world defines and the mind perceives through the senses has to do with form, like shape, size, color, sense of importance, etc. Form is temporary by its very nature. So if we think we are a form, like looks, body features, social status, intelligence, wealth, fame, etc. then "we" perish with the form, but if we go beyond the form and realize the heart of our being in the Spirit then we become what the Spirit is. Each one of us is a soul. The Spirit is immortal, and is the source of all life. When we (a soul) realize our perfection in the Spirit, we are enlightened.

The Spirit is God.

◊

Since there is now no condemnation at all for those who acknowledge their true identity in the Spirit, why shy away from accepting the present, which is life, fully despite all unpleasant events which happened in the past? Why let the finite mind rule over us? Why let the carnal mind rob us of the infinite potential that is in the Spirit? The mind identity is full of suffering, because the mind is the source of all needs, desires, and cravings. Yet the mind is never really satisfied, and therein lies the reason for the human misery. The carnal mind is like a monkey that constantly jumps around on trees, picking up fruits and throwing them on the ground or at others without enjoying the fruits. If you patiently observe the carnal mind, you will realize that it does not want to see others happy and neither is it happy on its own.

The mind is like a curtain that separates us from the

Spirit of God. According to the Bible, when Jesus died on the cross, the thick veil hiding the most Holy place in the temple in Jerusalem was torn in half. That symbolizes the spiritual avenue that is available to realize the most Holy place within us which is otherwise hidden by the carnal mind. Christ should not be perceived as our physical savior but rather our spiritual savior. If we wait for some opportune time in the future when Jesus will come back in a physical form to take the followers to heaven then we might miss Him. Jesus Christ is here with us in the Spirit because Christ is the Holy Spirit, the perfected state of our soul.

We all have the seed of Christ within us.

◊

Now is the time to humble ourselves, kneel down and confess our wrongs to whom we have wronged, and forgive those who have wronged us. We need to accept what is the reality, appreciate what we have, and do good regardless. By continuing in the old ways of the carnal mind, or supporting the status quo by building a mental defense system, we are only delaying what will eventually fall, be revealed, or cannot be sustained. We need to let go of the worldly strings tying us down, and be like a free flowing river with no resistance to the current. Sometimes the water level rises and sometimes it falls, but the river is the same regardless, season in and season out. What is gone cannot be brought back, and what is left is our life. *Let us live this present moment completely without anything pulling us back or bogging us down, without any fear of the future either; this precious moment that makes up a beautiful garland of life,*

and everything else?

Well, there is none!

A Pilgrim

What did I bring into this world that I long for so much?
What can I take it with me where no object shall I hold as
such?

From the light that I came, and to the light shall I return
The world is a maze to keep me enslaved and forgotten.

Bound by the carnal mind, the world is a wonderful bait
Lost in the abyss, countless souls gone through that wide
gate.

Stranger to the world, then known by my Father
This world is no home for a pilgrim, who then rests
thereafter.

2 BE CONTENT

*"***Godliness with contentment is great gain.** *"*
- 1 Timothy 6:6

In this age of mass media and mass marketing, it is difficult not to be attracted by the appeal of colorful and "sexy" ads. We are told what to eat, what to wear, what kind of bed to sleep on, and the rest of the unlimited shenanigans. We let our minds be programmed and thus our lives are affected by materialism and its inherent dissatisfaction. We become like androids rushing to get a new flavor of a coffee drink, or stay in a long line to get a new model of a smartphone. To the mind getting those newest things makes us happier, more complete, or more important. Often we follow the suit just to fit into a crowd and we do what everyone around us is doing. But then have we ever stopped and wondered why our life is not really happy or complete? Surely that must be so because we are constantly grasping at everything that shines before our senses, and we are plagued with uncertainties, worries, and fear.

If we have always tried to derive our sense of happiness from material objects because we were raised that way or we saw our parents try to win us with new gifts and presents each year when we were young then it is time to make an about-turn in our life and derive our sense of self from the Spirit of God. As we separate ourselves from the world and its ways, we see the futility in searching for happiness outside of us. We start to decipher the deception that is in the mass media. The Madison Avenue wants us to think that happiness lies in a new car, big flatscreen TV, polished food processor, chic purse, etc. so we can be sold those objects. Then after we have given into the temptation and bought a new toy, we realize that the sense of incompleteness is still in our heart. This is like a dog chasing its own tail.

◊

The issue here is spiritual. It is deeper than a sleek looking phone, car, TV, attractive woman, handsome man, or whatever your heart may fancy. Worldly things only reflect the spiritual void that is in us. When we were young children, we were amused by shiny and colorful toys, their shapes and sound. As we mature, we put away those colorful toys. But did we really put away the "toys," the sound, and the colors? The little toys only change to bigger ones. We keep longing for the newest model of a cellphone, for example. We become amused and happy like little children when we open up a new package, eager to play with our latest gadget. It is one thing for a child to play with toys as the child is immature and its brain young, but quite else for grown-ups to try to find a meaning of life in material objects.

Psychologically, our constant quest in acquiring material possessions reflects the primal need to be loved. When we were very young, our parents or primary care giver tried to fulfill that need. As we grow older we become more independent. However, the world is still the same; a wild place, and the future uncertain. So what do we do? The easiest avenue is what we already know, and that is to be amused with newer "toys," and try to forget about the scary and the uncertain world. The point here is that we are lost in the world with its glamor and glitz. We keep grasping for the wind until one day we wake up and realize that all the worldly sound and colors cannot really satisfy our soul longing, which is the need to be loved or be in oneness with the Spirit of God. Love is of the Spirit of God. The toys of the world then appear pale, dim, dull, noisy, and even meaningless.

We are like travelers stranded in this world, and most of us do not know that we are meant to transcend this physical world. We do not end with the body or the world. We walk back and forth on the same road of life every day, and we are tempted to take every new turn with its colorful billboards we encounter on the crossroads of life, while most of those new turns lead us to the dead ends of life. What we are truly seeking for is the way back home, our spiritual home, the place of eternal rest for our soul.

We are made in the image of God. The essence within us is the Spirit of God. When we are created, we are blessed with a soul (in a figurative sense because we are a soul). A soul takes this *samsaric* (worldly) journey to be perfected in the Spirit. The earthly realm of form is a part of the journey of our soul. We have the challenge before us to overcome this form realm. Form is perceived by the mind and its senses. To overcome form is to transcend the mind itself. Yet by ourselves we cannot do that because we are still in a form. A fisherman does not carry a boat on the water; a boat carries a fisherman on the water. It is only through the grace of God that our spiritual eye is opened. Everything happens according to God's will, and God encompasses everything.

"No one can come to Me unless God, who sent Me, draws him."

- John 6:44

◊

By us consuming more, we deny the Spirit from revealing in us. This is like clouds obscuring the sun. The sun always shines brightly, but clouds can make the darkest day. We deafen the voice of the Spirit by the noises of the world and by suppressing our soul calling with more worldly toys. Materialism is a quagmire to our true Self. That is why Jesus told a rich man that it is easier for a camel to go through the eye of a needle than for a rich man to enter the kingdom of God. If it troubles our heart to give others freely and we are only adding more stuff in our life then we are getting deeper into the worldly mire. Just think about this truth that *we brought nothing physical into this world, and we will take nothing physical with us when we leave this world*. Our body was formed with dust on the earth, and it will end up as dust on the earth. This world is a sensory labyrinth, a snare, for our soul. What matters is our soul and its karma.

"I am a sojourner in this earth. "

- Psalm 119:19

◊

Keep your expectations checked when you are dealing with others. Enter into acquaintance with no expectation, and that will save you from unnecessary disappointments. This fallen world is inherently selfish. Take your interaction with other people like when a noble prince meets a poor man; the prince is courteous and humble, yet when they depart, the prince does not feel burdened or disappointed. Just like the prince, if we have no expectation from others or this world then we can live and leave freely.

Do not expect people to be courteous or respectful to you. So when you encounter a rude or selfish person, you will not be bothered, and you will have the grace to pray for the person. Furthermore, understand that it is the ego in you which desires respect and honor. If you do not set expectations while dealing with people then you are immune to the disappointments that come from the unfulfilled expectations. For example, if a person expects to hear a hymn in a new church but is welcomed by a Christian pop music, the person may be bothered. But if the person has no expectation then even a concert like loud music in a church will not bother the person !

"When you are invited by anyone to a wedding feast, do not sit down in the best place, lest one more honorable than you be invited by him; and he who invited you and him come and say to you, 'Give place to this man,' and then you begin with shame to take the lowest place. But when you are invited, go and sit down in the lowest place, so that when he who invited you comes he may say to you, 'Friend, go up higher.'"
- Luke 14:8-10

The same goes for our relationships as well. When we enter into a relationship with too many expectations, there are more things to cause us dissatisfaction. Some people cannot find their "ideal" match because their expectations are too high. The Perfect and lasting match is impossible for the mind to find because once the mind knows a person, then the person loses his or her appeal to the mind, and the mind is consequently disappointed. It is as though the mind cheate d itself!

She will kiss a frog, but ignore a prince in front of her. He sang a sonnet and promised her the moon, but now he does not even pick up a TV remote.

We do not appreciate what we have by focusing on the things that we desire. As long as we are in this earthly body, there will always be something that we do not have and which appeals to our senses. So the secret to happy relationship is to try and look for the good qualities on the other person we are with.

You can talk to the other person you are with about the things that can be changed in him or her, or you can accept him or her the way he or she is. However, we should always put love before our expectations. Now for married couples, for things that are difficult to live with in their spouse which surface over time as they share the same roof, they can learn to cope and accept with patience and love. If you are struggling with an issue with your spouse then use prayers onto God to help you. Do self-examination first, oftentimes faults lie on us more than the other person. Be loving always, and gentle in your approach. Do not let any harsh word or a selfish action add fuel to the fire. *Compassionate words or actions always quench the fire of contention.* Do not let the carnal mind jeopardize your marriage.

Observe the mind next time you are with someone, and see how the mind tries to manipulate you in ways to satiate its needs and desires, even severing the tie with the other person if the mind thinks that the person is not worthwhile. The mind is constantly judging, and it is inherently selfish. People who are led by the carnal mind end up being lonely and unhappy. They may be able to get fame, fortune, or be with other men or women, but they become like a paper flower, spiritually dead.

Having no expectation does not mean that we become passive or like a robot. On the contrary, we are active and participating in whatever situation we are in. There are no strings of expectations over us which are pulling us down. So when we get something, no matter how small, we appreciate it even more. If we do not get anything then there is nothing to regret about. If something bad happens then we are not bothered as much. It is a fail proof guard for our heart and saves us from a lot of disappointments in life.

◊

Let your plans be anchored on your present circumstance or what you currently have. Living our life is like climbing a ladder; we get higher up as we step on each upper rung. If we wish to skip most rungs and get on the top of the ladder at once then we might just fall to the very bottom. A young bird that recklessly flies too high falls to the ground. We need to distinguish between having undue expectations and making prudent plans.

One is a path filled with disappointments, while the other is paving a new road to our "happy" future. Now, plans do not always come to fruition, but that should be the least of our concern. A wise man accepts failure as an outcome, and also understands that failure is not an end.

"For which of you, intending to build a tower, does not sit down first and count the cost, whether he has enough to finish it. Lest, after he has laid the foundation, and is not able to finish, all who see it begin to mock him,... or what king, going to make war against another king, does not sit down first and consider whether he is able with ten thousand to meet him who comes against him with twenty thousand? Or else, while the other is still a great way off, he sends a delegation and asks conditions of peace ."

- Luke 14:28,29,31,32

Forget about the worldly securities that we all desire. Think of the plans that you make today are not to make your future secure, but rather to improve your present circumstance. It is just a shift in our perspective, and it relieves us from putting our trust in the future, or our focus on things outside of us. Nothing that the world offers is secure or constant. There is a sense of relative security in modern technology, insurance programs, job skills, friendship, etc. However, they can only go so far. Apart from the security that comes from "knowing" our true Self, there is none in the world. A soul does not need material security, in fact worldly security ends up being a bondage to a soul. The mind needs the sense of security, and what the body needs is already provided for.

◊

Do not be grieved by other people's successes or achievements. Open your heart and rejoice with them. Doing so motivates us to appreciate what we have. *Jealous people are unhappy people, because in their jealousy they overlook their own blessings.* Love is an antidote to jealousy. We do not feel bad when our mother, father, or our siblings get a big promotion. Much rather we rejoice with them, and cannot wait to congratulate and hug them. As we open our heart and expand our circle of intimacy, we love more, and our happiness factor also increases correspondingly. Try it for yourself today. *When we are happy for others, happiness is all around us.* With love overflowing within us, we become like *"the salt of the earth."*

◊

We need to learn to be content with what we have no matter where or how we are. This is the secret to joyful life. Joy is not in the fulfillment of our desires, or possession of material abundance; it is not in being with a beautiful woman or a handsome man; and it is certainly not in a higher social status. If it were so then all the rich and famous people in the world would always be joyful. Yet that is clearly not the case since we occasionally hear of sad news of rich and famous people taking their own life.

Granted we get a sense of happiness when our desires are fulfilled, but that is only short lived. Yes we need our basic needs fulfilled. A hungry belly is not a happy belly, and there is no denying in that. However, if we analyze the mind, we see that it is craving for more, worrying about something that happened in the past, or fearing about some "possible" future event. We need to bring our mind to the present moment, and focus on what we can do to alleviate the current circumstance, if indeed we are struggling to get our next meal. Worrying is like a distracting smokescreen, and it never does us any good. No wonder worrying is considered a sin, as it is to doubt God about what God can do in our life. When our vision is clear without fear or worry, the mind is free to focus on the matter at hand more effectively.

◊

Instead of having a *needy* mentality, we need to have a lacking-nothing mentality. This is a shift from the mind representation to walking in the Spirit. The mind immediately focuses on an extreme scenario like, "I need food, clothes, money, and a place to live. Otherwise I will end up in the street and who knows what." What we need God provides, and it takes faith in God to let go of such doubts. To the mind it makes sense to doubt what is unseen, but that is an impediment to a soul. The carnal mind is always craving for something and looking for a sense of security. Even king Solomon with all his riches, power, and women strived for more, and towards the end of his life he acknowledged that it was all meaningless. The Spirit lacks nothing because it is the source of all, even life.

The carnal mind is very crafty. When we have resources to fulfill a desire then its appeal becomes weak. Just having an avenue to accomplish a desire creates a lowering effect on its temptations on us. A saying in Asia goes, "A carpenter's house lacks a good set of stairs." It is not that a carpenter lacks the necessary skill or resources to make a good set of stairs, but rather he does not feel the need of his work in his own house. This is synonymous to supply and demand principle in economy. When a supply of something is low, its demand or temptation is high, and vice-versa. So instead of dwelling in lack, internalize the truth that you, as a soul, lack nothing in the Spirit. The more you identify with the Spirit, the more you experience peace and joy in your life.

It takes practice to disidentify from the mind, and it is a good meditation. When we are tempted, sit quietly and instead of thinking about the desire being tempted, try to think that the desire is of and to the flesh. We are not the flesh or a feeling. The mind will try to reason, and convince even. However, that which is being tempted will go away. If we give into the temptation, we can not hold onto that feeling of fulfillment a moment longer, and what is the real gain? **Nothing** . If we do not give into the temptation, we still have our self like before. Yet, in a sense , we win because we did not give into the temptation and lose anything. Fulfillment of a desire costs something, either money, time, or some other resources, even social honor. When we are spiritually strong and able to see the futility in temptations, we are able to resist them. This frees us from any guilt associated with giving into the carnal desires, which is considered a sin in a religious context.

It is not a desire that is a culprit , but the carnal mind which creates the pull in us to a desire. Fulfillment of a desire is not a lasting solution, since it is like pouring water on sand. To overcome a desire is the lasting solution. This does not mean that desires will not come, but rather we are able to resist temptations. Temptations, which are still the same, lose their appeal on us.

Those who have overcome the mind have overcome the world .

◊

Happiness is a choice, but in order to make the right choice we need to be able to see our choices, otherwise we are mostly limited to unhappiness. Jesus started His saying with "Whoever has ears, let them hear ." when he addressed the crowds. That was not because the people lacked ears, but rather not everyone was able to get the right message in His words. In other words, choices are visible to us only when we are ready for them. That is why it is important that our will be aligned with the will of God for our life. *The mind is limited in knowledge, but the Spirit of God is all knowing.* When the mind is free of fear and worry, it is able to think clearly and connect freely to the Spirit.

What is meant for us, we will get it anyway, and what is not meant for us, it is better if we do not get it.

If we are happy with less then we will be happy when we get more. But if we are not happy with what we have right now, we will be unhappy regardless. That is why it is important to have appreciation for life and all its blessings. As long as our focus is in the future or in the past, we fail to enjoy the present. Besides, happiness is a relative term, and we can be happy in a humble sustenance.

Rather than thinking ourselves as an owner, we need to think of ourselves as a good steward of what we have. It is easy to enjoy our life that way. We should not cling to any material object or a person, so that they cannot make us unhappy. Even resist from clinging to any view, concept, ideology, doctrine, or dogma. Happiness is a state of mind, and it depends on us, rather than on others or the world. we can learn to be content right now, and consequently we find ourselves happy.

Do not seek worldly praises or honor. They try to

massage the ego, but the ego is never satisfied. The more praises we get, the more is desired, and that is an avenue for disappointment. The underlining root cause of our being attracted to praises and honor is the hunger in us to be loved and accepted. Now this desire to be loved is naive, but to the carnal mind pride masquerades and takes the vacant space in us which should have been filled with love. *Pride is a bubble that only gets bigger*. However, when we realize that we are loved by God unconditionally, we are set free from the compulsive desire of seeking praises, accolades, or even trying to force others to love us. Now some of you may be wondering, "When did I force anyone to love me?" Have you given a nice gift to someone with the hope that they will value you more or treat you with more attention? To the mind, it does not matter what avenue is taken as long as it gets what it wants. We become blind to the next person with our selfish ambition. That is why the world is filled with misery.

◊

When we let compassion move us, love seeps into our innermost being, *"the holy of the holies."* In giving love we are loved, and renewed in the Spirit. Yet love is always within us. We become more receptive or sensitive to love as we walk in the Spirit. We can love anything or anyone. There is no discrimination in love. Through our selfless actions we show love. He who has not shown compassion is farther from God, and though he may lack nothing in a worldly sense, he is poor. While he who is poor in a world but has love in his heart, he is rich despite his poverty.

We can all take time and contemplate on how we are loved.

Meditate on love. Start with the ones whom you love and those who love you; those who are close to you, your family, your best friend, even your pet.

Remove all expectations of them as expectations alienate love among people. Just experience love.

Remember of the fond memories, being together in the ups and downs in life.

I hope that you felt warm inside your heart, and you felt joyful. Yet even wonderful and perfect is the love of God. When we are able to feel the love of God, we are set free from all bondage because that love is all encompassing and empowering. That is the grace of God. There is no need to prove anything, and no compulsion in the love of God because we are already sanctified, complete, and strengthened by the power of love.

Life is Beautiful

Life is beautiful, precious in its special ways,

garland of moments adorns the one who has a cherishing

gaze.

how easy it is to live and not live at all

short-sighted by the distractions of this world.

ungrateful for the blessings we have, always craving for

more and more.

on and on until we hit the wall, but then we long for what

we had before!

we realize how wonderful this life is, all the blessings so

easily hazed.

*In this moment that holds the eternity, life is beautiful,
precious in its special ways.*

3 FOCUS ON THE POSITIVE

"For as he thinks in his heart, so is he."
- Proverb 23:7

No matter how much you have been through in your life and no matter how much you have lost in your life, there is always something worthwhile to live for in life and to build your life with. If we focus on negativity then the negativity will overwhelm us because the human mind is vulnerable to the spiritual darkness. It is like if we were climbing a mountain; to climb down is easier than to climb up because we act with or against the gravity respectively. However, when we focus on what is positive, we feel energized and passionate about life.

The mind can be liken to a radio receiver which responds to frequency bands as we tune it into a certain channel. There are lower frequency bands and there are higher frequency bands that a radio can tune into, and depending on a particular frequency a radio gets a certain feed. Now think of the Spirit of God as the field of Consciousness in the Universe, and depending on where we are spiritually we respond to the Spirit accordingly. Lower Consciousness is seen in the mind representation, where we are easily influenced by pride, anger, fear, shame, etc. Higher consciousness is the Spirit representation, where we are influenced by love, joy, peace, etc., which are the fruit of the Spirit. God encompasses everything in the universe, and the Spirit is (of) God. Everything that is is conscious, more so in a spiritual sense than in a biological sense. The field of Consciousness is the Spirit. In other words, Consciousness is God in essence.

The function of the mind can be compared to how a computer functions. If we feed negative input to the mind, it will spit negative output, and vice-versa. *For, as he thinks in his heart, so he does*. Garbage-In-Garbage-Out, or **GIGO**, as it is called in the computer terminology. Generally, what we surround ourselves with, we are influenced by that. Hence it is a good idea to filter what we put into the mind. All of these sound very obvious, but the reality is not so simple. Oftentimes, we end up doing what we know is not beneficial to us, and we fail to do the thing that we know is good for us. *Knowledge by itself is useless unless it is put into action*. This paradox of the carnal mind is succinctly expressed in the Apostle Paul's letter to the Romans.

"So the trouble is not with the law, for it is spiritual and good. The trouble is with me, for I am all too human, a slave to sin. I don't really understand myself, for I want to do what is right, but I don't do it. Instead, I do what I hate. But if I know that what I am doing is wrong, this shows that I agree that the law is good. So I am not the one doing wrong; it is sin living in me that does it. And I know that nothing good lives in me, that is, in my sinful nature. I want to do what is right, but I can't. I want to do what is good, but I don't. I don't want to do what is wrong, but I do it anyway. But if I do what I don't want to do, I am not really the one doing wrong; it is sin living in me that does it."

- Romans 7:14- 20

◊

If we think that we can lead a virtuous life by merely replacing one habit with another then we try to tackle our problems superficially. Habits, which are compulsive in nature, cannot merely be substituted for another. An untrained mind is bound by low spiritual consciousness or lack of spiritual consciousness. The carnal mind is like a falling apple bound by the force of gravity. The root cause of our habits is spiritual in nature. As long as we do not deal with our problems spiritually, we continue to face hurdles without getting much further, and consequently facing much frustration.

We should not discount the benefits of trying to improve our life by doing good. It can be abstaining from harmful substances, spending time in a positive activity, acquiring a new life skill, etc. Oftentimes, our good deeds become fuel to usher us spiritually into higher Consciousness by opening new doors in life. When love fills our heart, we are free from the need to find our sense of completeness in the worldly things or other people.

◊

When a child is born, the mind is immature, but the Spirit is shining forth. We can see the Spirit revealed in a heart melting laughter of a small baby. As we grow older, the mind starts to obstruct the Spirit, like clouds casting the sun. When the mind totally overshadows the Spirit, it is like a total eclipse of the Spirit in a person (Illustration in Fig 3.1). It is a tragedy for the humanity because the Spirit is all knowing, but the mind knows little (though it thinks that it knows a lot). The Spirit is infinite, but the mind is limited. The mind left on its own is like a termite infested log; eventually it brings destruction to the self and others.

Anything good in us comes from the Spirit; and apart from the Spirit everything in us is corrupt. What is corrupt eventually dies, and what is left is good. If we identify with the flesh, our identity dies with the flesh. Whereas when we are born in the Spirit, we are eternal. Try to distinguish yourself from the carnal mind. You are a soul. You are in a body, but you are not a body or the mind. For example, if you feel bad when something good happens to others or if you feel good when something bad happens to others, then the part that feels the jealous pain or callous pleasure is not you but the carnal mind perpetrating as you. You are not the mind. We, as the image of the Spirit, want to love everyone and all the time.

Fig. 3.1 *Total eclipse of the Spirit*

In reality the mind cannot overcome the Spirit; how can the moon overcome the sun? However, the mind can overcome this "I," the soul or our spiritual self. Try to grasp this concept for a moment. Imagine yourself as an air bubble in a level tool (Fig. 3.2). The air bubble moves left or right as you tilt the level. Similarly this "I" is identified with either the mind or the Spirit as we shift our focal point of being. Being identified with the mind is to be identified with form, like looks, body, job, relationships, social status, etc. Whereas being identified with the Spirit is to be identified with the essence, which is revealed in the manifestation of the fruit of the Spirit, like humbleness, generosity, altruism, love, joy, peace, etc.

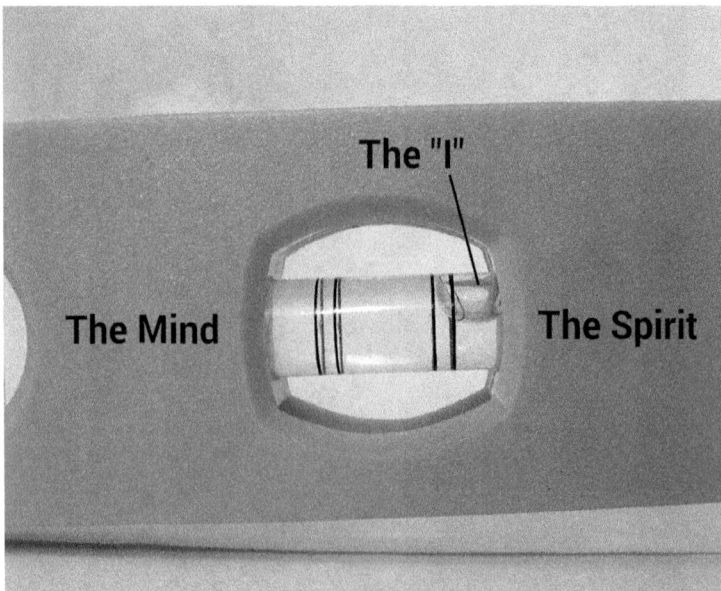

Fig. 3.2 *Bubble in a Level Tool*

Things are not absolutely black or white in the human dimension. This is because we are still in the flesh, and it is natural for us to identify with the mind. Idealism is the concept of the mind. The spirit is ideal, but we cannot be ideal according to the mind while still governed by the mind. We cannot force the will of the mind to the Spirit. Occasionally, we may get glimpses of the spiritual sun. Those are the "Ah" moments. We can try to play the perfect symphony, but we will miss some notes here and there. Life in this world is imperfectly perfect, and here in lies the beauty of our human frailty. In our weaknesses the strength and grace of God is revealed, for when this mind representation of "I" fails then that gives way to the true Self to be revealed forth in us.

◊

"For without Me you can do nothing. "
- John 15:5

By our own, if we can even say that, we are this body or the mind. A body constantly seeks to fulfill its needs and desires. The flesh is thus helpless. It is no different than other animals. Human DNA is very similar to that of other animals like Chimpanzee, and the cell functions are basically the same. The distinction between humans and other animals is more spiritual than physical. All creation inherently channels the Spirit in some ways, and yet only a human soul can transcend the mind to realize the perfection in the Spirit. Other animals are helpless because they are rather limited in their capability to transcend the realm of form to their perfection. Thus the flesh is not an end, and we do not end with the body or the mind.

We need to shift our focus from the mind to the Spirit.

◊

Everything in the Universe is happening accordingly. We cannot tell a plant when to grow; we cannot tell a bird how to fly; we certainly cannot tell cells in our body how to function. Everything is happening perfectly as it should in the creation. Imperfection is introduced with the carnal mind, because the carnal mind is inherently imperfect. It is quick to judge, and to compare and contrast. Just observe the mind; it is quick to point out the things that do not seem to "fit" according to its definition. That is why an opinion does not have much weight against other opinions, and we all have our personal opinions.

If we walk by the dictates of the carnal mind, we fall.

Even though the mind is imperfect, yet if it is disciplined under the Spirit then it is a perfect tool. True discipline comes when the mind is subjected to the Spirit. In other words, when the carnal mind is humbled, it does less of its selfish works and more out of love. When the will of God aligns with our will then the mind is much useful. We are all individually endowed with talents and gifts. When we are spiritually aware and walk in love, we are able to use those talents and gifts for the benefit of all. Impediments like pride, jealousy, selfishness, etc. are overcome as we walk in the Spirit. Our vision in life becomes more focused with the carnal distractions lowered.

◊

The Spirit knows everything because it encompasses everything. Even though the Spirit is not bound by time or space, yet the realm of form, which is subjected to time and space, is limiting and limited in its access to the Spirit. For example, the Spirit is always available on the earth, and the level of knowledge on the earth is growing with time as we unravel more knowledge. The important thing we need to know is that the mind is not the source of thoughts or ideas. A "new" idea comes from the Spirit or Godspace (explained in the next section), which further increases the level of knowledge in a particular domain.

In order to contribute to mankind, we need to be able to channel the Spirit, granted we may be led by the Spirit without us actively knowing about it. When we are led by the Spirit, we are open to other's concern and useful to others. However, the carnal mind can mimic others in good deeds. When led by the mind, the underlying factor is self-gain. With pride or greed as a motivating factor, our deeds end up being less productive even though they may have a big potential.

Whatever things are true, whatever things are noble, whatever things are just, whatever things are pure, or whatever things are virtuous (**Philippians 4:8**)

is from the Spirit.

GODSPACE

To walk in the Spirit is to be attuned to the Spirit. It is like we are connected to *Godspace* (like the term cyberspace to a computer terminal connected wirelessly). The author has a background in Network Engineering and some of the thoughts are influenced by the technical knowledge in the field. In this section, the author has naively tried to conceptualize God with the knowledge from his technical perspective, yet he acknowledges that God is undefinable. Besides, God is beyond time and space, yet as much in this realm. So the suffix word "space" is used just to convey the meaning of the field of Consciousness by its comparison to the word "cyberspace." Once we say, "God is this," then we are confronted with conflicting notions about God. Hence notions or concepts can become hindrance to us in our spiritual transcendence. However, the mind needs to "picture" an idea or a thought, and thus description serves our interpretation.

The idea of *Godspace* came about as the author

thought of the interaction of a computer terminal with the Internet. If we think of the Internet as always on, unlimited storehouse of information, and a powerful entity (which is happening ever so as more intelligent and powerful devices are connected to the Internet) then we come closer to understanding the concept of Godspace, granted that we are comparing apples and oranges here.

A computer terminal by itself is rather limited. One can prepare reports, do photo editing, surf the web, play games, etc. Though a computer may be able to do millions of calculations in a second (Million Instructions per Second, **MIPS**) on its own, yet the real power comes when it is connected to the cloud or the Internet. Just think about any smart device you use, like your phone, tablet, laptop, etc. What happens when a device fails to connect to the Internet? Though a computer can perform basic functions on its own, yet its real potential is realized when it is able to interact in cyberspace.

Now try to envision the Spirit as the all-knowing Consciousness, all encompassing, and all powerful. The moment something is in the mind, it is already registered in Godspace because we, similar to a computer connected to cyberspace, are a part of Consciousness. Nothing is hidden from Godspace; *every hair on our head is numbered* . Every action is accounted for whether it is seen by others or not. So the notion like "It is fine to cheat as long as we are not caught" is a self-justification of the carnal mind. This flesh is not the end of us, and had it been otherwise then anything would have been fair. "Eat, drink, and merry, for when I am dead I am nothing," so a worldly man thinks in his heart.

The mind is a powerful entity. We just need to look around to see all the modern marvels at work. However, analogous to a computer, when the mind is affected with the "**I**" virus, it becomes self-serving and very limited. It makes us callous, greedy, and "independent." As a child grows up, this "**I**" virus grows along, being nurtured by language, culture, and the society in general. The "**I**" virus limits our access to Godspace, just like a computer virus can compromise or sever an internet access. On a similar note, worrying can be thought of as Denial-Of-Service (**DoS**) attack in the computer terminology. Under **DoS**, a web page or an online resource is made unavailable by bogging down an online server with a constant barrage of service requests. When we worry, instead of thinking about a solution for a problem, we bog down ourselves by constantly thinking about the problem. **DoS** is taken seriously, and it is a federal cybercrime in the US.[1] But worrying, though detrimental to us, often goes unchecked in us.

The more we are able to channel Godspace, the more we experience joy and peace in our life. This is because joy and peace are the fruit of the Spirit. In essence, we are a vessel for the Spirit; and when this vessel is clean, it is much useful and blessed.

"I pour out myself, so God flows in me. "

In a spiritual sense, we become clean when we are not polluted by pride, falsehood, and a whole host of other attributes of the ego. Yet as long as we are under the mind, we are not liberated from the darkness of the ego. Consequently, there are few days when the sky is bright but many more days when dark clouds cover the sky.

The ego is our identity in the mind.

◊

Although we say God is within us as the Spirit, the essence of God is everywhere in the creation. However, to connect to Godspace we need to seek within ourselves. Idols and statues only serve as a reflection to a seeker, the real temple is the self. People who seek to please God with idols and rituals can only get so far. Yet that is not meant to discount any religious ritual. There are some positive effects in rituals which help us to be in-line in the Spirit, and cause the grip of the carnal mind on us to be loosened, whether in reverence or fear. But one should not settle with an object or a person for God because doing so is a spiritual blindness and a big hindrance to one's soul. There is a popular Buddhist saying, *"If You Meet the Buddha on the Road, Kill Him. "* This is not meant to promote violence, but rather to highlight the importance that the real Buddha or Christ is within us. We should not believe or settle for anything naively, which can otherwise lead us astray.

"Test all things; hold fast what is good ."
- 1 Thessalonians 5:21

It is important to have an open mind when we do not know where we are, nor where we are going. Yet we need to be cautious as well. Do not settle for the first thing that comes your way, nor anything colorful, extravagant, and majestic that tries to woo the mind. When in doubt, prayerfulness is always helpful. However, we need to have faith in God if we are praying to God. For example, when you ask a question in the Internet, do you trust that your query will be posted on a website for others to respond to? Or when you search for something in an internet search engine, do you expect to see some pertinent results? We will not feel confident if our queries are lost in a cyber black hole. We use technology like Internet search engine because it is fairly reliable. We need to have strong confidence in God, acknowledging that God is able to do what we ask for, should we expect to see a positive result in our life.

◊

When we look at the world and see how humans are swayed by good and evil, it dawns on us that the human quest, both individually as well as collectively on the long run, is to overcome the realm of the mind or this form world. For us to transcend the mind will be like for a computer to become aware of itself, like looking at itself from a human perspective (its maker). In a human term, this is *Enlightenment* . It is the opening of our spiritual eye and the realization of our true and perfected Self. We do not become someone new or something else, we become who we always have been.

Enlightenment is and brings a fundamental change in us. This is not a superficial understanding where we read about Enlightenment, and feel that it makes sense and then forget about it, like when someone takes a glance on a mirror, turns around, and then forgets the image. Enlightenment happens when we are ready for it. Flowers bloom, eggs hatch, women go into labor, and when our soul is karmically ready then the true Self is revealed in us. Again, time is no barrier to the Spirit, which is eternal, and the journey of a soul goes through the spiritual metamorphoses (or spiritual evolution) until it is perfected. Birth and death is only applicable in the realm of form. Furthermore, the journey of a soul is like a big game, where it completes a level and proceeds to the next level until it reaches the final level. Yet even that analogy is insufficient to describe the "impermanence" of the permanent.

The Christian term "born again" can be inferred to mean Enlightenment. It is used rather loosely in the religious context these days. The real meaning is deep, and it is the spiritual awakening in a person. This is different from being merely religious, reading a Bible, or being baptized in water. We cannot be "born again" by our own accord. It can only happen by the grace of God (when the heavenly treasure of a soul is ready).

This is reflected in Jesus's answer to Nicodemus in the book of John,

"The wind blows where it wishes, and you hear the sound of it, but cannot tell where it comes from and where it goes. So is everyone who is born of the Spirit."

- John 3:8

A small step goes a long way in the kingdom of God. Good deed, no matter how insignificant it may appear to the mind, matters. It can be picking up a trash on a road, saying a compassionate "Hello" to a stranger, choosing not to eat animal, forgiving an ungrateful friend, etc. However, we need to be cautious about not being led by pride while we do good. Such good deeds, leavened with pride, serve to massage the ego, which robs us spiritually.

◊

Even if you lose everything you have or the whole world forsakes you, yet you still have "You," your true Self. However, just because you have something, you may not realize it, and thus may go on living your entire life being oblivious of your true identity. Only our soul passes to the spiritual realm from this physical realm, but if we are not karmically ready then our journey in this form realm continues. Form can change, giving rise to birth and death, and a soul, which is not physical in form, continues in its journey to attain its perfection in (the likeness of) the Spirit.

Suffering can be a blessing in disguise, if it is able to humble us and to bring about the spiritual awareness in us. When a person loses everything in the world and there is nothing left to lose then either the mind overcomes the person or the Spirit overcomes the mind. When the mind overcomes a person, the person suffers from mental afflictions or even commits suicide. However, when the Spirit overcomes the mind, which happens when the self surrenders onto God, then the Spirit shines forth in us.

When this attractive world loses its colors and sound to us, we reach a point in life where we are able to feel that we lack nothing and also crave nothing of the world. This opens up an avenue for us to experience joy and peace regardless of our circumstance. In other words, whether it rains or shines, we have the spiritual sunshine of peace and joy within. That is what "knowing" God means. As we walk with God, God walks with us. We are of God, and although it may sound blasphemous, we are "God." In the spiritual sense, the whole encompasses one, and one encompasses the whole. There is no separation. But when the mind tries to grasp the concept about God, the ego takes over and that hinders our transcending the illusion of self. The carnal mind secretly thinks that it is "God."

Imperfection cannot realize perfection, just like darkness cannot overcome light. The ego is the imperfect self, and it is like a little leaven that leavens the whole lump. God is beyond the comprehension of the mind and all the concepts it comes up with. But then you may ask, "Why even bother in this topic?" The objective is to nudge readers to go beyond the concept, and experience God for themselves. An artist paints a picture, and a writer can write about the picture. Often we are able to envision a picture by reading a detailed description of it. This is like reading a book and then watching a movie based on the book, and realizing how similar the movie was with our mental "movie" while reading the book. When we imagine, we channel Godspace. Even thoughts come to the mind from Godspace. Thus telepathy is not unreal. It is like people searching for the same *keyword* in the Internet simultaneously, or an intuition when something happens to a family member and later being amazed about the intuition. Godspace is like a lake which knows about a small ripple regardless of where the ripple occurs in the water.

When it comes to a spiritual matter, it is rather easy to answer, "*I do not know.*" if it is ambiguous to us, and chances are that we will be confronted with questions whose answers are vague. Often it is like each end of a thread leads to a new yarn whose other end we do not know. Thus it is safe to use words like Omnipotent, Omnipresent, Omniscient, eternal, or attributes like love, just, good, righteous, etc. when we try to describe God, because these words are vague, immeasurable, or incomprehensible to the mind, and which are not untrue either.

◊

Having made the distinction between form and the underlining spiritual essence, we are in a better position to focus on what is positive. Otherwise our horizon is limited or shelled by the carnal mind, and consequently we hit a spiritual ceiling every time we try to climb higher. Good ethics is noble and helps in nurturing a principled society. Yet that can only go so far. What about the difference between a man and other animals? Animals can be trained to behave well. We are not robots either. *Thus we ought to focus on what is spiritually positive, which is beneficial to us individually as well as to others.*

We are all connected in the Spirit. In the spiritual sense, you, as an individual, encompass the whole, and the whole is encompassed in you. There is no separation between the two. Hence even a thought in the mind matters. Selfishness, pride, greed, jealousy, etc. exists where there is separation from the rest, and thus it has no place in the Kingdom of God. We do not envy ourselves, and neither are we jealous of ourselves. When we love other people, we show love onto ourselves. It is easy to love others, even strangers, when we realize that we are all one in the Spirit. Attributes like race, color, ethnicity, religion, nationality, and social or economic differences have no priority in love.

Love is deeper than the skin and further than the mind.

Spiritually speaking, when we help other people selflessly, we help ourselves as well because we are all one in the Spirit. When a poor person benefits out of our charity, it is not only the poor person who benefits but also this conscious realm which we are all a part of. On the other hand, any act of envy, cruelty, lie, hate, etc. serves to hinder or regress the spiritual progress in a person or that of the collective psyche or realm. Thus it is important to focus on what is positive so that we do not give into wrongful temptations and end up being further mired in samsara. Like tiny raindrops that fill up a big bucket, good deeds no matter how small benefit the entire universe.

1 – Legality of Denial of Service attacks (http://resources.infosecinstitute.com/legality-ddos-criminal-deed-vs-act-civil-disobedience/)

Life

Life is perfect in its imperfections

Many hopes are unfulfilled
many dreams are shattered
tears run down these eyes like a waterfall,
yet life is perfect in its imperfections.

Friendships turn into bitter enmity
laughter turns into mourning
this heart aches with the cooing of a thousand doves,
still life is perfect in its imperfections.

The more I get, the more is desired
the more I have, the more there is to lose
then a sudden gust sweeps them all away,
but life is perfect in its imperfections.

Youthfulness turns into wrinkles
friends all leave like fireflies at dawn
then I felt that I finally figured it all,
yes life is perfect in its imperfections!

4 FORGIVE ALL, INCLUDING YOURSELF

Peter asked Jesus, "Lord, how often shall my brother sin against me, and I forgive him? Till seven times?"
Jesus answered him, saying, "I say unto you, not till seven times, but until seventy times seven."
- Matthew 18:21,22

Forgiveness is for oneself, though it is usually directed towards others, usually to those who hurt us personally. Since it is usually directed towards those who cause us hurt or harm, we feel reluctant to let go of that carnal desire to retaliate. We get so easily motivated to get even with the offending person. In the mind we long to neutralize the hurt caused to us by inflicting equal harm to the other person. But if we look deep into those thoughts and emotions that take over the mind when we get angry for vengeance, we see that those thoughts and emotions only serve one purpose and that is to destroy everything, even causing more harm to ourselves. Just think about the last time you felt that strong desire to get even with a person for something that was said or done. What did your harsh words or reaction achieve when you acted on the impulse? More than likely you two do not speak to each other now, even though years may have passed by, and there is still that strong negative feeling for the person in you.

What is the benefit of vengeance? **Nothing** . In the spiritual realm, to give into vengeance is to give evil free pass in our psyche. Similar to letting a wild wolf in our home. In vengeance, those who lose suffer, and those who "win" also lose as they go down deeper into the spiritual darkness, which is the separation from God. The mind tries to convince us for its good in any situation. However, not everything that shines is gold. Since we readily identity with the mind, it is easier for us to be led by strong carnal emotions.

To be led by the carnal mind is to be estranged from the Spirit within.

◊

It is wrong to hurt or harm others whether it is done in the mind, or through our words or actions. Usually we are very sensitive to a hurtful comment from other people, but quite oblivious to our careless words to others. Yet just because someone said something cruel to us or did something wrong to us, does not justify our cruel words or wrong action towards other people. A wrong does not neutralize another wrong.

"Just as you want men to do to you, you also do to them likewise ."

- Luke 6:31

Evil is evil either way, both parties who give into evil are equally wrong. In other words, evil is evil no matter what form it incorporates; the evil essence is the same regardless. However, this does not mean that people who are carried away by evil emotions are evil. We all are vulnerable to the emotional ups and downs in our daily life. We need to clearly distinguish between the two, form and the essence. *Our focus should not be on the flesh and blood that we see through our physical eyes, but rather on evil which is pulling the strings invisibly from behind .* This way we are able to love our enemies, and pray for them who deliberately do us harm.

When we give into evil, though it may appear that we have triumphed over other people, the bad fruit of our evil deeds clings onto us. Thus the phase "End justifies the means" is a fallacy because this physical life is not the end of a soul. Those who give into violence eventually fall, though we may not see the karma unfolding in an immediate sense.

◊

"Blessed is the lion that the human being will devour so that the lion becomes human. And cursed is the human being that the lion devours; and the lion will become human ."

- Gospel Of Thomas , Logos 7

When we give the mind to a negative thought or an emotion of vengeance, we defile or corrupt our soul. The mind goes on an auto-pilot mode of ruminating on vengeful thoughts with malignant emotions spiraling in like in a whirlpool, thus causing a vicious cycle until we feel bogged down or even snap. If we continue to ride the vicious tide by thinking about negative thoughts then it can manifest in a physical ailment. Whereas, if we let the negative emotion go as an outburst directed outward, it may cause others harm. Some people may advise us to let out the anger by directing it to some inanimate objects, or by engaging in some other activities, like sports. They are fine, but we need to go deeper to tackle the root cause of an issue. By merely suppressing symptoms, negative emotions caused by a hurt in us will erupt in an ugly manner at an inopportune time. If we have any anger or grudge buried in our psyche, and we are willingly or unconsciously letting it roam within the mind like a wild animal in a zoo enclosure, then we need to let the wild beast of anger out of the mind, and release it far away from us. We do that by choosing to forgive others no matter what, no matter how big the hurt is, no matter how much damage is done, or how much anger we feel inside.

There are many examples of family members of murder victims openly forgiving the killer(s), and even praying for them. *It takes strength of the Spirit to do what is impossible through the carnal mind*. When we choose to forgive, we transform what is negative or the spiritual darkness in us into the positive light, which shines not only in us but all around. Thus, forgiveness is a noble choice, but we have to be spiritually ready for it.

Forgiveness is like a brake that stops a moving wheel. A person does something wrong to his or her family member(s) out of ignorance or selfishness, and the cycle of pain and suffering continues in the family. Everyone in the family suffers. Some call this a generational curse. It is rather tragic as young lives are affected, and they too continue in the same pattern of abuse and suffering. Karma takes its course, and yet with forgiveness we can end such negative recursive patterns. Forgiveness starts with us. It gives us the power and motivation to change the course of not only our life but also that of others for good.

If we feel angry towards someone, and we are not spiritually strong and able to let go of the strong negative emotion, then it is a good idea not to confront the person when the emotion is high. Let the storm of anger pass by.

Try not to call, send an email, or even gossip about the offending person. With time emotions ebb, and emotions like anger lose their strength over time if we do not constantly think about them. When we are emotionally composed then we can talk to the person who offended us or whom we have offended, and bury the hatchet.

◊

Do not hold a grudge against anyone. *It is not you holding the grudge, but the grudge that is actually holding you and keeping you in its captivity* . If we show mercy onto others, even our enemies, we fulfill multitude of good deeds. Unforgiveness is a hindrance which keeps us in the spiritual darkness and also restricts our blessings. In our blindness of unforgiveness due to anger, jealousy, greed, or pride, we become willing to sacrifice our own happiness to callously desire to see others suffer, which is giving into evil. When people give into evil, though they may prosper for awhile, they eventually fall, with bigger the fall over time.

Not holding grudge against others is having love onto oneself. If we understand that unforgiveness is bad for us then we are more willing to let go of it. We need to be able to love oneself first before we are able to love others. This love is not the narcissistic or the ego-centric adulation, but rather compassion onto oneself. Now you may ask, *"How can I have compassion onto myself? Isn't that way of thinking a duality?"* Not quite. Think of it this way, that compassion which you have for yourself is the love generated out of the Spirit within you to "that person" who is "you" when you are not able to forgive others. In other words, you will see yourself needing compassion when you hold onto a grudge. It is a mental concept because once you are able to forgive others then you are better than what you would have been. And here in lies the love of God which sets captives free so they can set others free as well. While forgiveness is not dependent on others, by us choosing to forgive and pray for others, we intercede and help others as well. *Prayers of a righteous man avails much* (**James 5:16**), and by us walking in love we become a righteous soul.

◊

It may be considered a folly to be ruled by the carnal mind and not being able to let go of a resentment. Many people will say such as, *"How can I forgive my enemy who spitefully used me and abused me?"* Yet in forgiving our enemies, we are letting go of the negativity within us. Just because most people react through the carnal mind and hold on to their grudge does not make it right, nor does all the approval from the society or our family make it right. *Two wrongs do not make it right*. Let the unforgiveness in you go, and feel the freedom available in the Spirit. You take the high way, the way of forgiveness, not the same old path of hatred, filled with broken bridges and desolate roads. Life is too short to live a dead life plagued with bitter poison of anger and malice within us due to not being able to forgive others or oneself.

◊

It is impossible to forgive others as long as we are being led by the carnal mind. Pride precludes us from being able to forgive others because forgiveness is a sign of weakness. Pride is diametrically opposite to humility. True humility comes from surrendering oneself before God because we acknowledge that this mind is helpless on its own, and we are nothing if it is not for the grace of God. Pride will fight tooth and nail to keep its turf, even denying us the opportunity to live a life free of fear, guilt, and shame. To the world pride is strength, and humility is weakness. However, in reality pride is not our strength and humility is not our weakness. It takes strength to say, *"I am sorry."* It takes strength to smile despite a broken heart. It takes strength to forgive others despite all the hurt inflicted upon us. That strength comes from the Spirit of God which is within and without. We can all experience the strength in the Spirit by choosing to love others, which involves forgiving everyone without any exception.

"A kingdom divided cannot stand." As such how can the Spirit within us be fruitful if we let the demons of unforgiveness rule over our heart? We need to stop being shortsighted by carnal desires, and experience the freedom and peace that is available in the Spirit. Let us

embrace God in the Spirit, through love towards everyone. It is so easy and so natural to forgive when we let love rule our heart. When we see others who hurt us not as our enemy but as a fellow victim of evil then compassion starts to erupt out of our being. When we are unbiased and patient, we have a better perspective to see how some people behave the way they do and how they cannot help otherwise. In our true nature, we cannot help but forgive and love everyone freely. *The Spirit is free flowing, giving, accepting, loving, joyful, and peaceful.*

◊

To the finite mind many things that happen in the world may seem unfair and even unbearably cruel. However, things happen as they should, otherwise why would they happen anyway? To understand this concept we need to look from beyond the point of view of the mind, which requires us to be just, fair, and neutral. The Spirit is not bound by emotions and feelings like the mind. Moreover, the Spirit is free from the confines of time, and so is the karma of a soul. The Spirit is not subjected to death, just like one's karma. *We are where we are due to our karmic propensity.* Seen from beyond the mind, the world is a constant interactions of karma.

Death of a loved one or someone who is a good member of a society is unfair and tragic to us. The word "death" itself is repugnant to the mind, for in it the mind senses the end of itself. This is rightly so because the mind dies with the body, and thus any death reflects the annihilation of the self. Now the mind is not a physical entity like a living body that we can experience it with the five senses, but it is an abstract entity of the human brain which encompasses the sense of our physical being. We experience the world through the mind, and we find or build our identity in the world through the mind.

Sometimes people find themselves in a situation where things do not make sense. It feels unfair, evil, and excruciatingly painful to accept their reality. In those situations people ask questions like,

Why do bad things happen to good people?

Why do good things happen to bad people?

Why do evil people go on doing evil?

Why does God allow famine, plague, or war in the world?

Why does God take away innocent children?

One answer that is common to hear for such questions is that it is due to the fallen nature of the world. While this answer is not untrue, it does not go deep enough to answer the questions comprehensively. When we try to understand the journey of the soul as it goes through the hills and valleys to its perfection in the Spirit, we are able to grasp the constant interactions of "sowing and reaping" that take place in the Universe, this grand play which encompasses everything. Luck or coincidence has no place in Godspace. It is due to our karmic propensity where we find ourselves at.

Even a seemingly bad event has a silver lining to it, and a seemingly good event has pain attached to it. However, when we transcend both good and bad or when we see things as they are through the unobstructed vision of the Spirit, then we escape the world of suffering and become one with the Self. This is Enlightenment or being "born again." This is the spiritual marriage when the two become One, a Holy union as a soul shines in the Spirit.

"When you make the two one and make the inside like the outside and the outside like the inside and the above like the below, and that you might make the male and the female be one and the same, so that the male might not be male nor the female be female, when you make eyes in place of an eye and a hand in place of a hand and a foot in place of a foot, an image in place of an image - then you will enter [the kingdom of God]."
- Gospel of Thomas : Logos 22

◊

We are the "prodigal son" who left the home and got lost in the world with its temptations, and through the bitter trials and tribulations of life and realizing the vanity of the world, we are heading back to our eternal home where our Father will embrace us, welcome us, and honor us, saying,

"You were (spiritually) dead and has come back to life! You were lost, but now you are found!"

- Luke 15:31

◊

"Beloved, never avenge yourselves, but leave it to the wrath of God, for it is written, "Vengeance is mine, I will repay, says the Lord."
To the contrary, "if your enemy is hungry, feed him; if he is thirsty, give him something to drink; for by so doing you will heap burning coals on his head."
Do not be overcome by evil, but overcome evil with good."
- Roman 12:19- 21

God is the ultimate judge, and nothing is hidden from the all-knowing Godspace. As such why even bother with trying to take matters into our own hand? Why add more sin over our head by acting on anger or self-righteousness? In our pride we become an obstruction to God's deliverance of justice onto those who are wicked. In other words, do not try to be God by being led by the carnal mind. God, like a hurricane, knocks down or uproots anything in the way of His justice.

Is this physical life an end to itself? People who

identify with the body, and thus think that they will perish with their body, live so selfishly to fulfill the needs and desires of the flesh. They do not care beyond this earthly realm because they are not sure if there is anything beyond this life. As such the physical death only serves to turn the wheel of karma again for their soul. Thus this realm of form, samsara, is never empty. Yet nothing is impossible for God, and God can wipe out everything and start all over again!

The mind can justify anything, but that does not make it true. Truth is complete in itself, and as such it does not need any justification. The heavenly balance sheet is always accurate and true. The all seeing eye of God registers everything. It is futile to try to act as God by forcing our justice onto others. God is perfectly able to hold all of His creation on His palm. So let us yield to God in doing His work. However, this does not mean that we become inactive or heartless. Always give love a priority, for God is not against love because *God is love*. The realm of form is a means for a soul to redeem itself. In other words, this world is like a purgatory for a soul.

What goes around comes around eventually, and what we sow we reap accordingly. This is a spiritual law. God's account is perfect, and God is just. Things may not manifest readily when we want to see them, but that does not mean that people can get away with evil things they do. Eventually the book is balanced. God is not limited by time nor space. However, things are not black or white as we like to think of them in absolute terms. This is where our forgiveness and the grace of God come into play. We have the ability to end the cycle of suffering and pain by choosing to forgive everyone, including ourselves. Thus, in a sense, when we walk in the path of love, we cease a soul's balance sheet from incurring further heavenly debt.

◊

Forgiveness sets us free from the prison of bitterness within us. No one in his or her right mind wants to be in any kind of captivity, yet we so easily give up our peace of mind to negative thoughts and emotions by letting them run in the mind or by acting on them. Pride is the main cause of not being able to let go of unforgiveness. Think about the countless friendships ruined, families separated, or wars caused by some egomaniac leaders. One has to ask if pride is worth the pain, hurt, death, and destruction. People get carried away by negative emotions only to realize afterwards that they hurt themselves equally, if not more, by giving into the darkness of evil. Forgiving is like pricking a big balloon with a pin; the pressure inside the balloon is released immediately, leaving us in the state of peace and freedom.

If we play according to the carnal mind then we will find ourselves lonely and miserable. This is the sad paradox of the ego as it wants to avoid being lonely and miserable, and even takes desperate measures to "win" people. But the egos are like the same polarity of two magnets, they repel each other. In other words, even though the carnal mind may be impressed by the extravagance or success of someone else, it secretly wishes to bring the other person down. The egoic friction can be readily sensed when two megalomaniacs meet.

What is gone is not you, what is left is what you live with. So let go of all the hurt inside of you for your own sake. Take a conscious effort this moment to set yourself free from the clutches of the past hurt by forgiving all, including yourself. It is easy to forget counting oneself. People can go on living their whole life by holding onto self-blame for a mistake that they made in their past, or for something that happened in their life or family. It is especially true in young people whose situation only gets worse as their personality is affected by not being able to let go of self-blame or the sense of helplessness. Not being able to forgive oneself can be attributed to introverted personality, solitude, social anxiety, or even suicide in extreme cases.

◊

It is human to make mistakes. No one among us is perfect, nor perfectly immune to making mistakes. We see a person on the television who is condemned of committing a heinous crime, and we may tell ourselves that we can never do anything like that. But we need to understand that most of those people who are condemned probably thought the same thing when they saw someone else on the television committing similar heinous crime. The ego does not like to think that it can ever fall. This is also a reason why many people who end up making a big mistake cannot accept their wrong. They avoid taking the responsibility for their action, and thus live in the state of self-denial. When we say that something is beneath us or that we are better than others then that kind of thought pattern is boasting and is the reflection of the ego. Human mind left on itself is capable of reaching a new low; you will be surprised! It is only through the Spirit that we can live "righteously"; otherwise, the righteousness of the mind is self-righteousness.

"Think not lightly of evil, saying, 'It will not come to me.' Drop by drop is the water pot filled."
- **Dhammapada verse 121**

Though humans are susceptible to making grave mistakes, yet there is no mistake so big that it is beyond forgiveness. If light can overcome darkness then love can transcend all hurt. Forgiveness is a choice, but it depends on the spiritual maturity in a person. Merely saying, "I forgive you" will not avail much to anyone if there is the lack of love in us. We can make others feel good by using kind words, but if the spirit behind the words is lacking then that will eventually show up in our action.

Let us not be miser with love, freely it is given onto us, and let us be like a conduit to God's love by letting it freely flow onto others.

◊

"He abused me, he beat me, he defeated me, he robbed me,.....," in those who harbor such thoughts hatred will never cease.

"He abused me, he beat me, he defeated me, he robbed me,.....," in those who do not harbor such thoughts hatred will cease.

For hatred does not cease by hatred at any time: hatred ceases by love, this is an old rule.

- Dhammapada verses 3-5

Forgiveness is up to us individually, and not onto the person who hurt us, nor even onto this world. We all make mistakes, and it is all part of our life. Who can say that they are good and blameless? So accept this basic foible of being a human, and forgive yourself for the mistakes that you have made, for all the harm that you have caused to others, for the things that you have done that do not make sense when you think about them now, and for the tears that you have caused to yourself, your loved ones, and others. Forgiveness is freedom, and freedom is life. Those who hold on to unforgiveness, fail to appreciate their life and everything that is precious.

Let Go & Be Free

Let all guilt and shame be washed off of you by forgiving everyone, and accepting yourself as a mother embraces her child despite all abnormalities that the child may have.

Let the love of God surround you completely as you open your heart with love for everyone, including yourself.

Lower the egoic defense created by the carnal mind, which is a big hindrance to the soul in realizing its true identity in the Spirit. Humble yourself.

There is nothing to feel ashamed of, nothing to lose, no pride, no jealousy, no judgment, no fear in love, and nothing necessarily right or wrong even; but just acceptance, compassion, joy, peace, and freedom through love.

Vanity Of The World

There once were three mighty kings in a land.

The first king marched the whole earth, and won
himself all he desired
then he died, he was forgotten soon after, but he was
still in the mire.

He defeated mighty kings, but when he died he was a
lost soul
His eyes were empty, his heart far away and cold.

He did not know what was to come, and what was
near was fear
he wanted to show his courage to those around, but
there was nothing left but tears.

They had a long procession for his funeral, and down

he went to his grave
oh how helpless is a body on its own! Worms eaten
unable to save.

Then I saw the second king rise up, and he went even
broad,
he acquired more extravagance, he called himself
"God."

Then one day he fell down his horse, and broke his
neck
in an instant he was reduced to a tiny spec.

Such is pride, easier to see on others, but elusive in
the self,
which makes us blind, unable to even ask for help.

Remember the third king? Well he is in us all, just
behold!
yet he who wins himself, though lowly, conquers the
whole world.

5 NO FEAR

"The light shines in the darkness, and the darkness can not overcome it"

- John 1:5

Living in the realm of form is filled with fear, as can be seen in all the words with "phobia" suffixed to them. This is because of the impermanent nature of form, and there is always that fear of "not being" or death. The mind wants permanence, and the last thing it needs is to accept that it will perish with the body. When we were young, we might have fancied that we would not get old like our grandparents. In a sense that was the mind keeping us away from acknowledging the truth about form, which is ephemeral. But as we grow older we start to see that we are just like everyone else around. This body too will grow old and return to the earth. Often, this realization in us brings about a shift within ourselves, which is seen as a type of crisis, for example mid-life crisis, crisis when faced with a terminal illness, bankruptcy, etc. When what we have trusted for our entire life caves in on us, we are left helpless to defend for ourselves. Yet despite the pain, it is an opportunity for us because we can make the paradigm shift about who we are by identifying with the Spirit instead of the mind. This gives us the freedom from the ways of the carnal mind which is the cause of our suffering.

Ultimately we overcome all fears when we realize that we are a spiritual being, and that even death has no power over us. Yet we cannot overcome the mind on our own because it happens by the grace of God. Death is only applicable in the realm of form as death is the separation of a soul from a body. The Spirit is eternal but manifests in form, just like water that flows in rivers and oceans takes the form of cloud, dew, or mist. For rain to fall, a cloud has to die. A seed "dies" (or loses its identity as a seed in the form) and then becomes a plant. Yet there is no death of water or a seed, and the term "death" itself starts to sound rather incomplete and even meaningless. Think of death as the absence of something because it transformed into something else, and not the complete non-being or null.

As we delve into this matter, we see that it is the

mind which is engaging in duality or conflicting notions, like here and there, good and bad, or life and death. Beyond the mind, everything is, and no-thing does not exist. There is an ever kinetic interactions taking place in the Universe which is not limited to the visible or the physical realm. The Universe itself consists of about 68 percent of dark energy. [1]

◊

Many people wait for "someday" in the future when they will go to heaven or be resurrected, and so many die in that belief as countless many have died with the same hope. The Bible says that *there is no remembrance of the Lord in death* (**Psalm 6:5**). If something is in the future, it will remain in the future until an effort is made in the present moment to turn it into our reality. We cannot live now and do something in the future. The present moment does not exist in the future, hence, any action ought to happen in this present moment.

The present moment is happening in a sense like a moving walkway in an airport. Symbolically, we live our life by stepping on a moving walkway. When we think about doing something in the future or looking back over our head in the past, we step aside from the moving walkway and let the present moment pass by. We need to have our hope of resurrection in the present, and not in some distant future. What we do now matters, no matter how small it may be. A kind word or a small act of compassion matters. Our good deeds remove the thorns on our path to Self-realization.

This life on earth is an opportunity to overcome the curse associated with form (corresponding to the negative karma of a soul). If we are not able to transcend the form in this life then the wheel of samsara rotates again for our soul. Time has no boundary in the Spiritual realm. It is only in the realm of form that we are limited to this sense of time and space. However, form is where one can wash the dirt of karma in order to advance to the next level in the spiritual journey until one's soul is illuminated.

◊

Having discussed the importance of the Spirit, we need to understand that this body is not nothing or this world is not nothing. Although in the eternal sense this life on earth would be reduced to next to nothing, yet that does not mean that the physical life is insignificant. A small seed seems obscure in front of a big tree, but that does not make a seed a bit insignificant. We are in this body, and this body is a vehicle to reach to the next realm in our spiritual transcendence. We are eternal, but these bodies age and die, and until we realize the perfection in the Spirit, we are governed by the limitations of the flesh. Thus we need to be responsible and do what is beneficial to and through these bodies.

Let us focus on the mind now. Fear as an emotion is real when we feel it in the body. The heart beats faster, the body trembles, it sweats, the mind gets on an auto-pilot mode gripped by fear and even goes "blank," etc. and all of these sensations are real when we experience them in the body. However, when we think more about fear, we see that most of our fears are based on the notion, "what if." For example,

> "**What** if I fail the exam?"
>
> "**What** if I am rejected?"
>
> "**What** if I lose this job?"
>
> "**What** if this house gets foreclosed?"
>
> "**What** if I end up alone and helpless in my old age?"
>
> "**What** if I die in an accident?", etc.

All of these questions are legitimate, but the problem with these questions is that they are based on the future, and as such they have not yet happened. They are only probable, and hence not a providence or fate. In other words, they may or may not happen.

The root of all fears lies in non-existence or death. Beneath the fear of rejection, losing our source of income, homelessness, or sickness is the fear of dying. However, there is no non-existence in existence, just like there is no darkness in the light. Life is existence (being) while death is non-existence (not being), so beyond the form death does not exist and it has no meaning. The Spirit that gives our real identity is eternal. **So you, as a**

soul, cannot die. There is no fear beyond the mind.

We need to distinguish between real fear and probable fear. Real fear helps us by cautioning us in protecting our body or what we hold precious. Real fear is often real-time or immediate. For example, the fear of heights while walking over the edge of a roof of a tall building is a real fear. The fear of heights keeps us away from going to the edge of the roof of a tall building. This is the self preservation. Whereas probable fears keep us captivated, nervous, and prevent us from living our life fully and freely. For example, fear of rejection can keep a man from being with a woman he likes, fear of poverty can push a person to take a desperate action, or fear of loneliness can fill a person's life with dread and depression.

Yet even "real" fears are not real, otherwise why do some people fear one thing while other people are immune to it? Or, why do we fear something as a child, and now we do not have fear of it anymore? Truth is absolute and not relative. Fear is not truth because it is a relative term. In other words, fear is a mind made sensation. Fear is like a distorted lens that obscures our vision. An object we look at is not a problem, but the defective lens that we use to view an object is the problem. When we correct the spiritual lens, we correct the distortion of fear and thus improve our vision in life. This is a good news because we can overcome fears that have dominated our entire life.

◊

Public Speaking & Fear As An Obstacle

Think of fear as an obstacle, like a hill, and when we overcome it then it is no longer an obstacle. Until we overcome fear, it is lurking within the psyche and surfacing when we encounter anything that triggers it. In order to overcome a fear we need to face the fear consciously, whereupon we let the light of Consciousness spread in the darkness that is fear. In a psychological sense when we practice on something that we are not comfortable with or what we fear of, we let the mind be reprogrammed so that it does not react with a sense of terror or crisis. In a way the mind is numbed to the fear as the brain is "hardwired" in reacting to a situation in a more conducive and positive manner.

This small section is focused on public speaking as it is one of the biggest fears in us. If we want to overcome the fear and anxiety associated with public speaking then we need to familiarize the mind with public speaking by practicing to speak in front of others. Take it easy as you try to condition the mind. For example, feel comfortable speaking in front of a mirror by yourself first, then practice speaking in front of your family or close friends whom you are comfortable with, and thus expand your horizon.

Familiarity of a topic is important in public speaking,

and hence the preparation. Also having some idea about your audience helps in your preparation. The point is that you want to remove as many of the surprise factors as you can. Also as you feel more familiar and comfortable being in your own skin, you feel more confident about public speaking. Self-confidence is different from pride, although pride can masquerade as a cocky self-confidence. Pride is phony, and it is not your strength. Thus overconfident people fall hard. We can be self-confident and yet be humble, and that is, indeed, a good combination.

Be comfortable in your own shoe.

Do you feel awkward when you look at your own photograph or video? Most people do, and listening to or watching our presentation is a good practice to condition the mind in becoming comfortable with public speaking. Looking at our reactions can be helpful in desensitizing the mind so we are not as concerned about what other people think or say about us. Listen to a recording of your speech or watch a video of yourself speaking, and impartially try to overcome any anxiety, fear, or concern that surfaces. If you notice a mistake, take it easy. It is alright, we all make mistakes. Catch the mind as it tries to avoid confronting the fear, and consciously bring the mind back to the listening or watching. *The carnal mind is very elusive and slippery.* Breathing deeply helps in the concentration. As you practice this, you will have a better

idea about your strong points and where you need
improvement.

While climbing a hill, we may feel tiresome and even
discouraged. Be open and willing to pray to God for
courage and strength to continue in your endeavor.
Oftentimes, we feel that challenges are bigger than us,
and that's when we need the strength in the Spirit.
Remember that the Spirit in you can work wonders
through you.

To Sum Up

Inaction is a big problem when it comes to public
speaking. Be willing to participate in any opportunity
you get. Join a local Toastmaster group.

Resist all temptation to procrastinate.

Remember that there is no failure, unless you bring
yourself down.

Let go of the overt self-consciousness, and take it
easy. Often we are very critical about ourselves.
Remember that people are usually not that critical.

Mistakes can and will happen, and yet you can
gracefully lead a presentation to a successful
conclusion. Do not have all or nothing mentality.

Always remind yourself that you are not trying to
impress other people with your oratory skill. Let your
focus be in helping others. When our driving factor is
love or concern for others then we are able to

channel the strength available in the Spirit.

Above all, be humble so there is no place lower to fall.

◊

Fear is like an uncharted territory. We have fear until we consciously step on it. When we make a move to face our fear or to walk on the face of fear, we start to take back its turf, granted it is not easy for the mind to face its own fear. However, when we mindfully step on that uncharted territory of fear, we realize that fear is not really there because it has not been there all along, it is the mind playing a trick on us. In other words, fear is a mirage of the mind. However, to the mind it is real, even though it is an illusion of its own making. For instance, as you sit in the comfort of your room, close your eyes and think about the fear of heights. Imagine yourself walking along the edge of a tall building, and know for yourself that fear is by the mind, of the mind, in the mind, and to the mind. When you open your eyes, you are in the safety of your room. A good example is the fear we feel when or after we watch a horror movie. The movie is a fantasy, and so is the fear. Yet some of us feel hesitant to look under our bed at night after we watch a scary movie. Moreover, many of us have woken up from our dream with the fear of falling down from sky. The sensation of the fall is surreal, and our body reacts accordingly with rapid heartbeats, body parts movement, sweating, etc. But the dream was in the mind!

When you are confronted with fear, breathe deeply, and do not let the fear control you. With patience and practice you are able to make more rational decision to improve any situation at hand. *Fear clouds the mind and our judgment*. A nervous mind under fear is ready to fight or flight. Much of what we face in our daily life is not life and death situation. Yet, regardless, the carnal mind often responds with "red flag" emergency like there is no tomorrow. We have all experienced regrets for our rash decisions, careless words, or mindless action we gave into because of fearing a fear itself.

Meditating On Fear

Consciously try to feel the emotion of fear in the mind as you sit quietly and breathe deeply. Watch the mind calmly. Know that the Spirit of God within you is greater than all fears.

Do not let an emotion take the mind away to some fantasy land. If you get distracted, bring the mind back to breathing consciously.

Without judgment or reasoning, feel the emotion of fear as the mind and the body react to it. Like a surfer, ride the emotional wave of fear. The negative energy of fear is lost as you practice this, just like a surfer loses the fear of big waves with practice.

Be aware that you are present in this very moment as you experience the emotion of fear. Just like if you were chewing an almond or a resin and after chewing for a while it is reduced to paste. Meditate on an emotion of fear until it loses its strength and it is overcome. Now, this is often easier said than done. It can be that we end up worrying instead, and let the fear overwhelm and overcome us.

Take it easy, do not force yourself. Let the Spirit move you as you try to loosen the grip of the mind by focusing on your breathing. If you feel overwhelmed then feel free to take a nap or a stroll in nature. However, do not let that short recuperation be your avenue in avoiding an unpleasant emotion.

Prayers help to shift our focus from the sense of helplessness due to fear to the sense of empowerment due to our faith. Prayerfully surrender an emotion of fear to God.

Shift the focus from yourself and the problem to something else that is not related to the problem itself. Be careful, however, as people find it easy to momentarily forget about their problem using alcohol, food, drugs, shopping, sex, etc. If you like you can shift your focus to God and entrust your problem or fear to God. This is figurative in sense, yet helpful none the less. Instead of saying, *"How will I go through this excruciating situation?"* remind yourself that, *"God is able to help me go through this situation, and He has watched over me so far."* The mind under emotional storm is helpless, and like a river charted by gravity, the carnal mind takes the option that it finds good which is not necessarily beneficial to us, and thus it ends up causing us more pain instead. However, in God is power, and no storm is too big to overcome the Spirit in us.

Whether it is through meditation or facing your fear with action, make it a practice, and do not be discouraged if you are not able to overcome fear soon enough. Go with the flow in the Spirit. The natural tendency of the mind is to avoid fear, or to resist you from shedding the light of consciousness over the darkness of fear. This is because of the egoic nature of the carnal mind, which is intrinsically fearful. The mind will rather avoid any unpleasant emotion than face it. So, for the carnal mind to assist you in dealing with a negative emotion of fear is stymieing itself. That is why the carnal mind is a bondage to a soul. So do not be naive as to look at the carnal mind for help, it is utterly helpless. In keeping us blindsided, the carnal mind is not only keeping us in the state of terror but also robbing us of the opportunity to live freely.

◊

Do everything you can to alleviate your present situation, but do so ethically and without hurting your conscience. Do not be hasty in your decision. Do not procrastinate and let things pile up either, which only makes matters worse, and consequently the mind ends up being overwhelmed by more worries and fear. The carnal mind likes to avoid things until it is unavoidable, and oftentimes it is unbearable. In other words, manage your circumstance so it becomes easy on you, and your life becomes relatively comfortable. If we have a little sense of order and comfort even in an excruciating circumstance, we can have a sense of hope and happiness in life.

Try to do one thing at a time and do not let "time" bring you down. Do not spread yourself wide by trying to do everything or please everyone. Every book starts with the first chapter, every first chapter starts with the first page, every first page starts with the first paragraph, and every first paragraph starts with the first word. *So take action, because if you do not make the first move, you never know if you will succeed.* Furthermore, success is not everything in life. We can achieve something worthwhile and yet be unsuccessful from the worldly perspective.

We all make mistakes in life and no one is an exception. For example, when we are writing a book we make many typos, grammatical errors, disconnected thoughts, and so on, but should that keep us away from writing? Mistakes need not define us, no matter how big they may be. Though the society can label us for our past mistakes, we can either yield to such societal judgment or overcome barriers and prove that the social labels are wrong. Granted that it will be like moving against a fierce wind, but the other option is to give up or give in.

◊

Prioritize your time so that you can focus on the most important matter at hand first. The mind likes to compartmentalize and organize things, so it is easier if we play by the rules of a game. As we get busy with our personal and professional life, it is important that we prioritize matters so we fulfill other's expectations upon us and still have time for ourselves. Above all have some time to sit in peace and relax daily, preferably in the morning and in the evening, even if your schedule is clogged up throughout the day.

Our soul hungers for the spiritual bread, just like our body hungers for the natural bread. Do we feed trash to the body when it gets hungry? Yet when our soul feels the spiritual craving, we feed ourselves with more junk. We sit in front of a TV for countless hours, go shopping to fill up our overstuffed closets, drink more alcohol, eat more, watch pornography all night, etc. Our soul hungers for love, joy, and peace in the Spirit. The world cannot give them to us because the world is in utter poverty when it comes to the spiritual food. The good news is that the spiritual food is free, always available, and in unlimited measures. However, the egoic cloud can block our access to the free supply of "Vitamin-D" of the Spirit.

◊

Do not think in your mind, "I did this" or "I did that," whether it is good or bad. If we think like that then good accomplishments will add pride in us, while failures will leave dents in our self-confidence. Think of yourself as a vessel which can be used by either the forces of darkness or the power of light. When we are humble, we welcome the Spirit to use us and strengthen us. *Darkness spreads in the absence of light.* Pride is darkness that pushes a soul away from God. Besides, fear is attached to pride because pride is never complete, always needs propping up, and ever wearisome of falling down.

Mind identity is plagued with fear.

◊

What we fear has a tendency to manifest itself. This is because of the power in a thought or a word. When we think about something, we goad the mind on that. With repeated thinking on something, it is like digging up a channel in Godspace. The mind is naive and acts on what is fed to it, and so it is vulnerable to negative thoughts of fear. For example, if we are afraid of a rejection from a potential lover, and we play the ugly scenario of being rejected over and over again in the mind, then our actions (or inaction) will be influenced by the fear in the mind.

There are infinite number of things we can be afraid of, and thinking of all those things will limit us from going anywhere outside of our house. The point is that the mind thinks of what is in front of it, just like cattle eats hay put in front of it. We can improve our situation by focusing on things that are beneficial and separating ourselves from negative thoughts, thereby making every effort to think positively by actively filtering what we put in the mind. Realizing that the mind is like an innocent puppy which goes after anyone calling its name or offering it a treat, helps us to recognize a sense of responsibility in actively guarding the mind.

◊

The reflection of the carnal mind can be observed in our daily activities. We like to buy new and shiny objects and throw them away when they look older or outdated, even though they may be fully functional. We like to associate with livelier crowd and healthier looking people. Buried within these inclinations or actions is our fear of death. Think of death not just as an instance of dying. To the ego, being forgotten, lost, or alienated from others is synonymous to being nothing or death.

The egoic mind constantly needs assurance that it is alive and in control. Do you find yourself constantly seeking approval from others? Do you constantly try to impress others? Do you enjoy feeling important? Even in our pious works, we tend to be led by the egoic mind. On the surface of these actions we see pride, but within them is the constant striving to keep the engine of the ego running by feeding it with anything that helps to affirm its sense of control and life. So, in a way pride is a defense mechanism of the carnal mind because without pride the mind ceases to be egoic, or the egoic sense of "I" dies!

The carnal mind wants immortality, and interestingly it thinks that it is immortal. Hence it does not want to deal with anything pertaining to death. The mind urges us to turn to a different channel when we see something gory on TV. We are reluctant to visit an Emergency Room in a hospital. We feel hesitant to go to a secluded neighborhood at night. We can observe the fear of death in these circumstances, though subtle. However, we are not talking about the mind conditioned in violence because it can readily commit any violence. Yet even then, those who commit violence do so to keep their ego alive, though at other's cost.

The ego is really very miserable, and those who identify with the ego are miserable. The ego is constantly fearful, never completely satisfied, never really appreciative of life and its blessings, always jealous of others, always craving for more, callous to other's suffering, and willing to take a risk at anyone's cost or even sacrifice oneself. Thus if we walk by the dictates of the carnal mind then we find ourselves unhappy and miserable.

◊

"We can easily forgive a child who is afraid of the dark; the real tragedy of life is when men are afraid of

the light. "
- Plato

In our attempt in drowning the mind with TV, music, books, partying, alcohol, drugs, sex, sports, politics, or even religion, buried deep within these lies the fear of death. We dread loneliness and separation from others because for the mind they are the harbingers of death. Yet any superficial measure only serves to remove the symptoms, whereas the spiritual void within us is never filled by worldly measures.

The spiritual void or the separation from our true essence is death itself, though not in the sense we perceive the term "death." Worldly things help us to momentarily numb the "pain" in our soul, but no worldly thing can fill the spiritual chasm. Any attempt with alcohol, drugs, women, etc. only takes us further away from God. The Spirit has always been within us because the Spirit is our soul identity. We are made in the image of God, and thus we are a part of God. The spiritual void is the emptiness as perceived by the soul (us) when the mind takes us away from God. That is why we need to separate ourselves from the mind. It is futile to try to tackle the issue created by the mind while still being identified with the mind. Fear is the reflection of the mind identity, because fear is an inherent nature of the ego.

◊

With fear being the fruit of the carnal mind, we can try to pry open a "room" in the mind where fear is "said to exist." We can do that by asking, "So what?" to our circumstance to see what is propping it. Oftentimes, we are like little kids who are afraid to look under a bed at night. When we go deeper in the crevices of the mind with courage, we realize that beneath all fear is the fear of death or "not being." Fear of losing a job, being rejected, falling sick, etc. all have the fear of death underneath them. Yet death is only applicable in the realm of form, and to the Spirit it has no meaning. How can water and oil mix?

Form changes, but the Spirit is eternal and the same . Once we truly acknowledge that we are not the mind or this body, and that we are an eternal soul, and this physical realm is a phase to bring about our illumination through the Spirit, then we start to experience freedom from all fears. However, that realization has to take place in the core of our being. In other words, the change in us has to be inside out. When we know who we are then there is no need to be somebody else, and there is no fear or worry in trying to be somebody else. This is freedom, and we are able to experience peace and joy because they are in our very being.

The flesh is no match for evil, and evil is no match for the Spirit. However, the point of interface is the mind, and it becomes like a tug-of-war with the Spirit on the one side and evil on the other side. Since we are still identified with the mind, we find ourselves helpless to evil and the ways of the flesh. Like a river that flows on the course already charted, the carnal mind leads us by the forces of its desires and needs. *Life is an uphill climb being identified with the carnal mind*. Only through the spiritual awakening in us that we can be free from the suffering and pain associated with the carnal mind.

◊

To walk in the Spirit is to walk in love, because *God is love* (**1 John 4:8**). If there is only one way to God then that is the way of love. In other words, love is the means for our Self-realization. No man can take us to God, and do not trust an angel to carry us there either. God is not here or there because God is everywhere when our spiritual eye is opened. Besides, love is an antidote to our fears. When we are perfected in love, there is nothing to fear.

"There is no fear in love; but perfect love casts out fear, because fear involves torment. But he who fears has not been made perfect in love."

- 1 John 4:18

Fear is a sign of lack of faith in God. To "experience" God we need to show love to everyone and everything, everywhere and every time. Love is the way to the perfection of our soul. People search for God in temples and churches, in thick religious books, in sermons, and some even look for God in the Sun or constellations, but God is often missed in the plight of a fellow human being, in calls for mercy from a repentant enemy, in the inane killings for a political or religious ideology, or in the senseless exploitation of animals or the environment.

Change starts from one soul,

and

you are a precious soul.

1 - http://science.nasa.gov/astrophysics/focus-areas/what-is-dark-energy/

Heart of Love

With no love, heart is just a flesh, beating and beating like a desolate island, with tides crashing and crashing.

Full of anger, heart is a furnace, fire burning within like a violent storm, causing destruction there in.

Full of envy, heart is a wild beast, sparing not even a close friend like a raging flood, devouring everything good till the end.

Full of fear, heart is a prison of iron like a venomous snake, quenching the soul with its deadly poison.

Full of apathy, heart is a tall wall, with no gate

like a total eclipse, blocking compassion with hate.

Full of treachery, heart is a ruthless evil, lurking in the
dark
like a sudden lightning, striking with no regard.

Full of lust, heart is a bottomless pit, with no end
like an insatiable hunger, ravaging everything with no
gain.

Full of Love, heart is the garden of Eden
walking with God, peace and joy within.

6 DO GOOD NO MATTER WHAT

Love is the bridge between God and man

Doing good no matter what is walking in love. Doing good is not dependent on our age, health, wealth, or social position, because the will to do good comes from the Spirit within us. We can find a rich man who is miser while a poor man who readily shares of what little he has. We can find a leader of a country who is corrupt and holds for himself what he has not earned, while an ordinary person in the same country who, despite poverty, selflessly serves others. Doing good is a choice, but that choice comes when we are spiritually ready. It is self-empowering and self-enlightening to say "yes" to do good in any situation, no matter how small or even opposing our action may seem to the conventional social norm.

Sometimes doing good is not easy, it is painful even. Yet, under such circumstances, the alternative to doing good is to accept being in the same stale state governed by the carnal mind with its bitterness of jealousy, greed, and pride. When we show our willingness to do good in modest circumstances, choices are made available to us to do bigger charity. Hence, if we wait for that special occasion in order to show our generosity then that break may come and go, but we may fail to notice it. New doors open up when we open the door right before us and we walk in in love. When we are humble and willing to be led by the Spirit of God, we please others as well as God.

LOVE

Love is the fruit of the Spirit. It is reflected in selfless action towards others. So to say "I *feel love*" is a misstatement as love is not a feeling. Much rather, we feel compassion towards others. It is also a misstatement to say "*I love you*" because that does not really mean anything as love is (in) an action.

Love is usually mistaken for a mental emotion or a lustful attraction.

Love is shown through our action, and all words are vain. Even praying in love is an action.

Love is not a need, want, or desire.

Love cannot be boxed, hold, or quantified. Contrary

to the popular saying, love is something we cannot share either.

Love manifests in an act of compassion, and is felt in a doer with a feeling of joy, which is an affirmation of the connectedness with the source of life.

Love does not discriminate, but rather brings us all together.

Love does not retaliate for injustice, it seeks to release others from the bondage of hate and anger.

Love sees others as oneself, and motivates us to treat them like we want to be treated, with respect and compassion.

Love is happy to see others free, while the mind wants to keep others bound to us.

Love is not a "thing" just like God is not a "thing."

Love is a state of being. So I cannot "have" love, much rather, I "become" love.

Love is not possible through the mind because it cannot love as it is inherently selfish. The mind seeks and reasons, and as such it is not a conducive environment for love.

◊

Love is unconditional, and as such it is not dependent on anything or anyone. One can say that the care and affection shown by a mother to her new born baby is love. However, the maternal bond is due to the natural relationship, which makes the care shown by a mother to her baby conditional. Now, this is not meant to portray the maternal affection as selfish, but rather to clarify unconditional love. Many things that happen in nature, though benign, appear selfish. A fierce lioness that kills a small antelope is caring and affectionate to her cubs. Yet there are also examples where a fierce lioness or a female leopard which killed a baboon was caring and affectionate to a small baby baboon. [1, 2]

Unconditional love is seen in a simple greeting to a stranger. This is not a perfunctory "Hi" said to someone we meet in a park to appear social. Take out all the expectations and obligations from your daily dealings with other people, and then love will surface in your actions. In love there is nothing to prove and nothing to be other than who we are. We just need to let go of all the carnal desires in us for others. With love our heart is open to other people, no matter who they are, rich or poor, famous or condemned, or clean or filthy looking.

Love does not have to make sense, even if the society thinks it otherwise. Thus loving our enemy is strange to the mind which is reflected in the society. There is no separation in love, and it is all we, us, or ours. Even in being charitable to people in their desperate needs, the carnal mind tries to seek something to barter "love" for, which can be praises or accolades from other people. For example, we have the carnal urge to take pictures showing us helping others. However, there is no spiritual blessing for us when pride hijacks our charitable deeds. We have to be careful not to be led by the ego because it leads us astray even in the most pious occasion.

◊

God & God's Love

God's love for us is unconditional.

God's love is shown in fairness to all. It is because of our individual karma that we find ourselves where we are. Yet the creation itself is constantly changing, and therein lies the fairness of God because there is always an avenue for our redemption. This is the *grace* of God.

God's love is manifested as the strength we have in the Spirit. Spiritual fruit is readily available, but we have to be ready to realize it.

God is not a Santa Claus who only brings good gifts to us.

God is like a good gardener who tends a beautiful garden full of rose plants who does not remove thorns from the plants. Life is like a garden of roses with thorns; sometimes we pick the roses and other times we pick the thorns. As we are able to see spiritually we pick the roses. God does not stop us from picking the thorns, though God warns us. Our ability to hear or/and heed the voice of God depends on us and not on God. This illustration is similar to the parable of a dragnet that Jesus told in **Matthew 13:47- 50** in which the dragnet is the spiritual awareness which enables us to separate good from bad.

God is like a big satellite on the orbit broadcasting down to the earth. We are like receivers. We are able to hear God clearly when we "face" towards God and when there is no worldly interference or obstacle in between.

God does not take sides with certain people because then that will make God a liar, but God is truth. So, the phrases like "My God," or "God's people" are fallacious.

God uses us to show love onto the world.

◊

Doing good is like sowing good seeds which bear good fruits. Eventually our good deeds do good onto us. But we shouldn't do good with any expectation at all, otherwise it becomes transactional or selfish, and we fail to spiritualize our charitable action. When we do good, it can be seen from two different perspectives; worldly one and the spiritual one. Good deed is good regardless as someone will benefit from it, and yet when a good deed is edifying to the soul of a doer then that is spiritually empowering to the whole. This is reflected in Jesus's word in the sermon on the mount.

"Take heed that you do not do your charitable deeds before men to be seen by them. Otherwise you have no reward from God. Therefore, when you do a charitable deed, do not sound a trumpet as the hypocrites do in the synagogues and in the streets, that they may have glory from men. Assuredly, I say to you, they have their earthly reward. But when you do a charitable deed, do not let your left hand know what your right hand is doing, that your charitable deed may be in secret; and God who sees in secret will bless you openly."

- Matthew 6:1-4

The biblical equivalent of the word *karma* is "sowing and reaping." A Buddhist thinks "sowing and reaping" in a wholesome perspective which involves multiple rebirths to escape the carnal world or *samsara*, while in Christianity faith in the blood of Jesus Christ sets people free from the bondage of sin through the indwelling of the Holy Spirit. Going beyond religion, the main point here is that good deeds matter not only in the immediate sense but also in the eternal sense. This is what storing treasures in heaven (**Matthew 6:20**) or adding good *karma* is about. We are saved by the grace of God, and with the indwelling of the Holy Spirit, we are able to do good regardless.

Love is 'natural' for someone who is born again.

If God were to judge us today, we would be judged for our deeds. Yet these terms are figurative in sense, and are illustrations for the mind. We are already judged when we do good or bad. Nothing is hidden from the universe of Consciousness which is God, and nothing escapes God who is just. God is not limited by time; each moment stands eternity and the eternity stands in a moment to God. We may not see karma unfolding in our timetable, but that does not mean that people can get away with what they do.

This book is not about religious debate on whether the Buddhist, Christian, or Hindu belief is right. All of them are not necessarily wrong. In spiritual sense, paradoxes become reality. For example, if people change their way of life positively after accepting Christ and are motivated in walking in love then their soul is being renewed in the likeness of Christ. Otherwise, merely attending a church for an hour every Sunday will not open any pearly gate. This does not contradict a different belief where people acknowledge the divine presence of Atman (Self) in them and they do good with the hope of their soul being enlightened or going to heaven. Oftentimes, the differences are in our perspective, such as the Holy Spirit being poured into a self, or the true Self being revealed in us. A glass can be half full and half empty at the same time, though they may seem contradictory to the mind.

If animals have excuses for being entrapped in this

cycle of suffering in the world then a carnal man has an excuse as well. But no excuse is any good as none is redeemable for anything. It is only through the grace of God that we are able to overcome the cycle of suffering in this samsara. In an epoch, only few are spiritually born (again) and make it to the other shore. So even if we lose everything we cherish in the world, it is incomparable to losing our soul in samsara. The world is a big maze keeping us all mired in the cycle of sin and suffering.

◊

How do you worship God? Do you face a certain direction and bow down or kneel? Do you chant elaborate mantras? Do you burn a candle or an incense? Do you sing and praise the Holy names of God? While all of these activities help us to be attuned to the Spirit and show our need of God, yet the better way is walking in love or doing good no matter what. When we alleviate someone's pain or suffering, we please God. When we uplift someone's day by treating the person with respect and compassion then we please God. When we do anything we can to preserve and protect life and the environment that supports life then we please God. With our altruistic deeds we please God. Yet this is said in a figurative sense because there is no God in the sky who smiles at us like a human. God smiles through other people when our deed helps them, or when we see the prosperity of life and environment around us. When we understand that we, individually, are connected to the whole and the whole is connected to each of us, then it is relatively easier to love a stranger and even pray for an enemy.

There is no better worship of God than charity onto others.

If we believe that God is pleased by rituals and traditions that have no compassion in them then our views about God are at fault. Such rituals and traditions are dead without any spirit in them, and those who observe them are no more than crowd pleaser who are in the spiritual darkness. Apostle Paul wrote in **1 Corinthians 13** that even if we donate all of our goods to feed the poor and give our body to be burned but have no love then our deeds are in vain. The point is to emphasize the importance of love in what we do, because our deeds are either motivated by love or else the ego. Walking in love is being led by the Spirit because love is the fruit of the Spirit, whereas pride, greed, jealousy, etc. are the fruit of the ego. Pride is not only personal, but it can be social as well, like race, language, nationality, ethnicity, culture, etc. When people hold onto their dry rituals or traditions just because they were born in a particular society and they want to preserve their cultural or religious heritage, then that reflects social pride. Regardless of our personal or social disposition, pride is a mire that keeps us captured in the ways of the world.

Salvation is personal. If a society becomes a

hindrance to us in realizing our true essence, it is better for us to forsake the ways of the society or the society itself. Jesus said to His disciples that anyone who wants to be His disciple will have to hate (or forsake) his or her own mother and father, wife and children, brothers and sisters (**Luke 14:26**). Jesus went even further in **Matthew 5:29-30** when He said that if our body part causes us to sin then it is better for us to cut off that body part. Jesus was speaking in a figurative sense to emphasize the importance of our salvation. When compared to our spiritual freedom, this body or this world seems minuscule. This body and the mind should be tools to our soul, and when the mind is under the Spirit then our soul is free and we do the will of God. Thus, the human quest, both personal and global, is to transcend the limited mind, and become God conscious.

◊

A prayer inspired by love has power. It has been said to ask in prayer of what we need, and yet if we are attuned to the Spirit then we really do not have to ask for anything because God already knows about our needs. No thought is hidden in Godspace, the consciousness is omniscient. As a soul grows in the Spirit, we are able to move accordingly as the Spirit prompts us. Things seem to fit perfectly like in a grand jigsaw puzzle, as miracles unfold around us which we were either oblivious of or otherwise took for granted. We do not have to strive or struggle when we walk in the Spirit. When we are spiritually aware, we see God's masterwork at play all around. Everything just happens as it has been happening before we walked on the earth because everything simply is. When we are "in sync" with the Spirit, we are like a cog perfectly placed in a grand clock which is always on time.

We perceive the physical reality through the mind, and there are infinite "realities" of the mind which are apart from our "reality," and yet everything is happening accordingly in Godspace. The Spirit leads us where no mind can go. Those who are enamored in the carnal mind cannot see beyond the mind perceived world. The spiritual knowledge sounds foolish to some, while many think that it is profound and thus for only ascetics, and many more are not able to go beyond the words. So let us pray in the Spirit, but pray for others who are in need, for those who are still in the darkness of the world, and for those who are helpless in the flesh.

◊

Our good deed should not be dependent on others, otherwise that is like a business transaction. Charity is unconditional, and it is done out of a loving heart. If we do good to get other's approval then we seek to massage the ego by looking charitable. When the ego takes the credit for a good deed, it ends up becoming vain for our soul. However, good deed is good regardless. Is our charitable deed edifying to the soul, or is it consumed by the bottomless ego? When our words or actions are influenced by love, they are good to all. *The hand that gives charitably is kissed by God.* This is the beauty about charity that the doer is blessed, and more so spiritually.

We should choose to do good to anyone and at every opportunity. *When we do good to our enemies, we have no enemy*. For by love, anger or unforgiveness is overcome. As long as we are identified with the mind, forgiving our enemy is impossible, because the carnal mind wants "eye for an eye" and "tooth for a tooth." It is only when we choose to invoke love within us, whether in prayer or through self-realization, that we are willing and able to let go of the fiery grudge and anger in us. A "God" who promotes equal retaliation is a "God" of the mind. Violence never resolves violence (in the spiritual sense). It may seem like a solution in an immediate sense by taking matters into our own hand, but when the seed of violence is planted then it brings forth the fruit of violence to us. Whereas, God is beyond the mind and promotes love, joy, peace, and harmony for everyone.

Mercy is better than justice. Sometimes we hear about a family or relatives of a victim of murder speak out in the news saying that the deceased will only be able to rest in peace if the person committing the crime is sentenced to death. Such views, though logical to the mind, do not speak for the soul of the deceased person, but rather are the desires in the people who speak them. Part of the reason why people think that way is because if the person committing a crime did not face the equal fate then that will be injustice. But who can escape the justice of God? By us choosing to forgive others, we are letting go of the bitter poison of anger and grudge in us. Social justice may happen, but we are not concerned about the justice of man. Isn't it worthwhile to see life being transformed, and a soul being delivered out of the darkness of evil? When we are in an emotional and spiritual turmoil, it is rather we who need the peace and freedom found in forgiveness.

God does not rejoice in the death of anyone nor takes pleasure in a single soul mired in hell, but rather rejoices when a person is delivered out of the bondage of sin. Sin is the condition of being identified with the carnal mind, and thus any action of the flesh (the ego) is sinful. We are all accountable for what we do in this body. By us forgiving our enemies does not mean that we are voiding their negative karma or condoning their actions. Rather, we are helping ourselves and others with the freedom from the bondage of the carnal mind or the world.

The key to heaven or hell is in us. For when we identify with the carnal mind, life is full of suffering and thus hellish, but when we identify with the Spirit, we lack nothing spiritually and thus our life is a bliss. In other words, heaven is the state of our being in which we are perfected in the Spirit, and hell is the state of our being in which we are completely separated from God. However, the mind's definition of heaven and hell can be quite different. A person can have all the worldly luxuries but be in an extreme pain of deprivation and loneliness in the soul.

Sometimes we want to do good but we feel hesitant because we are afraid of being taken advantage of. For instance, we are concerned that a poor and hungry looking panhandler at the side of a busy street may be deceiving us. While that may be true, but our good deed is not dependent on the other person. We help others regardless, and if a person is a liar then that person is answerable to God. Our good deed is never wasted. It may be that God uses us so that justice can be imputed on wicked people as they heap more bad karma for themselves.

◊

In a sense it is very easy and even intoxicating to enjoy the ride of pride. Pride is so pervasive and even natural to us when we are identified with the mind. Our good and charitable deeds are not immune to being hijacked by pride. When we say, "I did this" and "I did that," then we are being led by the egoic mind. This "I" representation is a big hindrance to the Self, which is the unobstructed soul identity. However, when we give glory to God and acknowledge that God used us to accomplish good, then we are able to let go of the carnal need of pride.

God can use anyone to do His will. We are not special in that sense. We should feel fortunate when we are able to wash other's feet, for many will walk away from serving others. Worldly people are too busy, do not see any benefit for themselves, or think it is demeaning to stoop low, and even if they help others then it is not unadulterated with pride. We ought to feel blessed when we are able to bring happiness to the faces of the neglected and those scorned by the society, for then we have become the messengers of God. We should not let the society do our thinking, nor our family members, not even the most learned one, and certainly not the mass media. We ought to rejoice when we are mistreated for doing good and misunderstood for walking in love, for then we have become not of this world but of heaven.

"Stranger to this world, yet loved by God."

◊

"In the multitude of words sin is not lacking, but he who restrains his lips is wise ."

- Proverbs 10:1

Few Words

We should be kind with words because they are powerful.

One careless word can estrange family members or best of friends.

Our words should be few, because the carnal mind

likes to exaggerate and tell tales.

Our words can win us new friends or make more enemies.

Kind words can quell a riot, while reckless words can incite a mob.

Being silent is not a sign of weakness. It is rather a self-discipline and thus shows strength in a person. When Jesus was being humiliated and struck upon by the guards after He was taken into captive, He was silent but not weak. Those who are insecure need constant reassurance to make them feel important or to prove their point. But those who have overcome the carnal mind sees vanity in praises or false accusations. For those who have overcome the world, their soul is secure and their heart is at peace despite any emotional storm in their life.

◊

A small key can open a huge gate. A good deed, whether it is our intention, word, or action, is not insignificant. We do not have to travel around the world seeking to do good, although that is noble; we do not have to spend all our fortune to do good, although that is generous. If we see a little worm struggling on a road on a hot day, we feel compassion for the worm and we gently move it to a shade on a grassy surface, we have done a good deed; if we feel bad because animals have to be slaughtered because of our food habit and we choose not to eat meat, we have done a good deed; if we hear a gossip and choose not to spread it any further, we have done a good deed; if we see a beggar in the street and we help him, we have done a good deed. An opportunity to do good is all around us and at any time; we just need to be willing to make a move and take the first step in walking in love. It is not the destination we should be concerned about but rather the journey itself. For the one who walks in the Spirit is already spiritual, and their soul perfected in love.

Having said that, we should not be judgmental or prejudicial towards those who do not follow or practice what we do. Otherwise that will show darkness in us. We should be loving always, and praying even, though in our heart, for the positive changes in others. However, until we are not absolutely sure in our soul about where we are going, we should not try to influence others, let alone drag others in the path. We should never assume that we know what is good for others and try to act on their behalf because we will be acting God then. We are all individually in this journey called life, and change happens when we become ready.

◊

Good morals help us lead a virtuous life in a society, yet the will to lead a virtuous life ought to be spiritually grounded. If we try to live a virtuous life on our own, then despite our best efforts we will fail. This is because we are identified with the mind and we are easily gravitated to the needs and desires of the body. We may try to look virtuous, but what is in the darkness eventually comes out. However, when we channel the strength in the Spirit then we move according to the Spirit, and we do good no matter what.

Some Good Advice

Do not lie or cheat. God is truth, and when we lie, we let the carnal mind obstruct the Spirit of God in us.

Do not give into sexual immorality, doing so quenches the Spirit of God in us.

Do not over indulge the body, doing so strengthens the grip of the carnal mind on us.

Do not commit any violence against anyone or anything.

Do not let any thought of revenge push you away from God.

Do not curse or speak ill of others. Do not gossip.

Do not do what the intuition says is wrong, oftentimes it is the voice of God guiding you.

Always be willing to help others in need. God uses us to do His will. Think of material wealth as not exclusively "mine." Be a good steward to the blessings from God, ready to help anyone, anywhere, and at any time.

Always be willing to show mercy onto others, even those you consider your enemies.

Always try and be humble.

Always honor life.

Feel free to add more to the above list, and try to internalize one advice each day in your life through action or meditation.

1 -http://voices.nationalgeographic.com/2014/04/03/baby-baboons-dramatic-encounter-with-lions-ends-with-a-heroic-twist/

2 - http://dailynewsdig.com/wild-leopard-adopts-baby-baboon/

Take Your Stand

Chasing the emptiness of the flesh

>>> *is wasting time in vain*

temptations only leave us in the earthly mesh

>> *on the winding road to nowhere,*

>>> *filled with pain.*

Greed is satisfying to the tongue

>>> *lust is alluring to the eyes*

seeking only pleasure does us wrong

>> *cravings of the flesh are sin in disguise.*

Hear these words of wisdom, ye all

>> *if you sow in the flesh, you reap death*

take heed to this wise call

if you sow in the Spirit, you reap the
eternal wealth.

This world is a battlefield these eyes unseen

there is a war for our soul in the mind

unless you are born again, you cannot win

remember! your precious soul is on the line.

The choice is clear, the decision is yours

will you take the stand or go along with the
world?

Choose it right for God does not want a soul to purge

as the body eventually dies, the soul shines
like precious gold.

7 TAKE IT EASY

Everything is happening accordingly, just relax.

Our life, no matter how complicated it may seem to us, is still manageable and enjoyable. We need to focus on the positive no matter how faint it may seem to us. If we go on looking for faults or reasons to be unhappy about in our life, we will find many such reasons and our mind will constantly think about them, thus making our life even more miserable. It has been said that happiness depends on our perspective on life; whether we see a glass half full or half empty. Yet to see life through the optimistic lens, one needs certain spiritual clarity. Now, spiritual maturity is different from mental maturity, being active in a church, or spending time reading a religious book. A person can be spiritually awakened, and not be "spiritual" in a conventional sense. *If we appreciate what we have and respect life, we have a sense of spirituality.*

We need to take it easy in life, loosen up, and not worry. There are infinite things that we can worry about, but life is too short for such short-sightedness. Besides, worrying does not do us any good. It causes us to lose our hope, fills us with fear and bitterness, and takes us away from God. We need to understand that ultimately God is in charge, and the best we can do is let God do His work. When we go through life's hardship, we need to know that our suffering is not hidden from God. There is always a purpose in events that happen in our life. Things do not happen by accident, and there is nothing called coincidence or luck in God's vocabulary. We need to develop patience as we wait for a situation in our life to change, which then helps us with perseverance in life's trials and tribulations. Hardship in life is like a furnace that softens us, refines us, shapes us, and makes us better.

Happiness is our choice. However, if we are not able to see our choices then we end up as if we had no choice. Whether we count our blessings or blame others for a tragedy in our life depends on us. If we are wearing perfectionist lenses then we need to take them off. Life is not perfect as we want to think about it. Life is constantly changing, and we ought to be adaptable to life. If we hit a wall in our life, are we going to just sit there playing a victim, or are we going to get up and climb the wall or walk around it? Life will certainly not wait for us!

◊

Life on this earth is finite. Our days comprise of limited number of moments, though many. Each moment holds infinite potential. In other words, each moment has eternity buried into it. Each moment has the seed of Enlightenment. Each moment has the potential to change the course of our life, whether for good or for bad. When people are spiritually awake, they intuitively understand the importance of living each moment mindfully. Living consciously is the awareness that comes when we are led by the Spirit.

Once we are introduced to *mindfulness* , we need to practice or incorporate it in our daily life. Mindfulness is a Buddhist practice which helps in Self-realization. When we walk, we are aware of each step; when we eat, we are aware of each chewing; when we talk, we are aware of each word; when we mediate, we are aware of each breath. Every touch, sound, taste, smell, sight, and mental feeling is elevated by the addition of the consciousness of the Self. As we are divorced from form and we identify with the Spirit, we become more than a passive doer of an action.

Living consciously means to be conscious of each thought in the mind. We need to be alert about the mind like a watchman who guarded a city in the biblical times.

What we put in the mind can manifest in some way through us. When we guard the mind, our words are prudent and our actions are beneficial. A wise person is vigilant, and is selective of his surroundings. This does not mean that we become exclusive, which implies pride. We should be open to others, but be selective in what we receive from others. Jesus hung out with tax collectors and prostitutes, taught them and helped them, but did not let them influence Him with their lifestyles.

Body Awareness Meditation

You can do this meditation pretty much any time, even in bed before you sleep and/or after you wake up. This helps us in instilling the truth that we have a body, but we are not this body or the mind.

Sit still in a quiet environment (you may lay down on your back for this meditation) and relax. Close your eyes for concentration.

Be aware of each breath, in and out.

Be aware of your body and feel the life energy in the body parts, starting from the crown of your head down to the soles of your feet, moving slowly and feeling each body part (or a set of identical body parts) at a time with the mind. You can spend like fifteen seconds at each stop as you focus on your body part through the mind's eye. This is like scanning your body through the mind.

◊

Just because something went wrong for us, no matter how big it may be, does not mean that our life is marred forever. Life will occasionally throw curve balls at us, and no one is immune to that. Yet we are resilient in our nature to face any adversity in life. We are like a forest that springs up again after a wildfire. Just look back in your own life about how you have gone through life changing circumstances, or look back in the recent history of mankind and see how countries devastated by wars or natural disasters have been rebuilt successfully.

Do not think that there is no more hope for you when something awful happens in your life. When we were little children, we played with our toys and when those toys broke, we asked for a new one and most of us got a shiny new one as a replacement. We see that same childish attitude in us when we make a mistake and we wish that our life will just miraculously revert back to some earlier point in life where everything seemed normal. However, if we were to analyze our life, we would realize that our life is not so perfect after all. Life is a cacophony of happy and sad moments, a roller coaster ride indeed. To them who expect too much from life, life ends up being unhappy after all, and to them who learn to take it easy and enjoy each moment, happiness is a way of life. We need to have a thankful attitude towards life, and be kind to oneself.

We find happiness in life when we are content with

ourselves first. People who are constantly seeking, craving, and grasping, for them happiness is a fleeting glimpse. Even when they get what they desire for, the sense of gratification is only short lived. The desire for the worldly needs is like a hot burning fire in a worldly person which cannot be quenched by more fuel of the worldly objects. Material consumerism only promotes bigger cravings in us. However, bigger is not always better.

When we take it easy in life and have a humble attitude, we are less likely to be bothered by a failure and we are able to take "no" for an answer. We learn to enjoy what we have and we work for what we need. We see greed, jealousy, pride, anger, and lustfulness bring about unnecessary headaches in life.

◊

Everything in this Universe is happening accordingly. The sun comes up each morning from the east and sets each evening on the west; tree leaves spring up, change color, and fall; rivers flow day in and day out; birds migrate to a distant land; even cells in our body are functioning accordingly as they should. None of these need our permission nor do we have any say on them. Everything simply is, and everything seems perfect until we try to exert our opinion or force our will on what is. To let God do His work is to take it easy in life. Life is easier to live that way.

God has provided enough resources to fulfill everyone's needs, but when we try to over-consume or hoard resources in greed then we introduce conflict in the natural system. When very few people in the world "own" much of the resources on earth and thus leaving the rest of the population competing for meager resources then we see conflict in the world system. Greed is more lethal than famine or war, for it not only kills millions of people through war or famine but also the souls of those who have fallen to avarice.

When we walk in the spirit, we have the realization that this world and everything it offers is vanity. We are still in the physical body and the body has needs. Yet everything that a body needs is already provided for. We need to stop looking far into the future with fear, and see what we are missing in this present moment with courage. This very moment that we are living and breathing. *We do not worry about this present moment, we worry about the future*. Yet God's miracles become obvious when we are in a desperate need. People get surprised when a stranger walks up to them and offers the help they needed. Nothing is hidden in Godspace, and our needs are not hidden either. God uses us to show love onto each other. Oftentimes we need to open up and let go of any inhibition in us. A small friendly comment or a smile can bring about fluidity in human interactions to accomplish the will of God.

◊

We need to be thankful for the blessings in our life. The spirit of thankfulness is a sign of appreciation for life itself. There are many things in life that you and I can be grateful about. Yet we take so many things for granted, even life itself, when we abuse our body with toxins, neglect, or reckless risks. Being able to breathe without a machine is a blessing; being able to eat without someone feeding us is a blessing; being able to walk, see, talk, taste is a blessing; being able to live freely is a blessing in itself; having a family who love us is a blessing. Just think about the millions of people who are not so fortunate, who only have few days or few hours to live, or who are alone and desperate. We are blessed, more so and in many ways than we usually think or acknowledge.

Human mind is very selfish. It will even deprive us of life if it cannot get what it wants. Think about infatuated young people hurting themselves or even committing suicide after being rejected by their sweetheart. We need to be careful and alert not to be led by the carnal mind. Life is too precious to barter for careless adventures that the ego likes to risk in order to feel alive or be in control. When we let go of the need to feel "somebody" by saying no to deriving our sense of importance from other people or the world, we are less likely to gamble with our life, our family, and everything we hold dear.

Human nature is motivated by scarcity. We appreciate things more when we have less or none of it. But it does not have to be like that for us. However, we need to train the mind, and we can do that when we realize that the body does not need more, and the soul lacks nothing. As long as we are identified with the mind, we always lack something because the mind is never completely satisfied and always incomplete. We only need to look at our closet to realize how much we are entangled in this world. We hoard things that we do not use, and yet we cannot let go of those things. This is a tragedy in itself because life becomes congested with more distractions, and thus becomes lifeless. We need to learn to let go and take it easy in life so we can live peacefully and have joy in life.

◊

Do not try to defend yourself in an argument. Know that you are a part (a son or a daughter) of God, and that views, opinions, or words of others cannot ever define you, unless you yield to them. Meditate on that truth so that you are able to deflect all negativity directed towards you. When we do not defend the ego, we are free from carrying the heavy burden of the false representation of the prideful carnal mind. Even if something bad had happened in your life that you did not have control over or just happened recklessly, let go of all the need to prove yourself innocent or right to other people. We all make stupid mistakes for which we feel silly afterwards. However, when you are wrong, acknowledge your mistake wholeheartedly so that you are less prone in making the same mistake again.

If other people think ill of you because of something in your past then you will be playing according to them if you try to defend yourself. *When two egos clash, they both lose*. By us trying hard to prove ourselves right, we play by the carnal mind, and as such we may be able to convince few but then we prop up the ego, and that is a fallacy in itself because the ego is the root cause of the problem. By us choosing to separate ourselves from what others think or say about us, we elevate ourselves up spiritually. *Silence is not acceptance, just like humility is not a weakness*. When we are not bothered by comments or criticisms of others and we are confident in ourselves, we have peace in our being.

◊

Try to find humor in a circumstance you are in. This is not meant to sound funny or bring attention to oneself, but rather to relieve the mind from being stagnant with negative thoughts. When we let ourselves loose and take it easy in life, we divert the mind from darkness to light. Although having a positive attitude may not be a solution of our circumstance in itself, yet it can be a good distraction when we are in a difficult situation. Oftentimes, we just need to have patience and wait for a possible solution to surface. However, when we let the mind drag us under the storms of our life, we may fail to take a proper action. We can stop a hole in a dam with a finger, but only when we are able to see the hole early on.

Having a sense of humor does not mean that we become insensitive to a situation, but rather it becomes our personality. As the wise king Solomon said in the book of **Ecclesiastes** that there is a time for everything. *A time to get serious and a time to take it easy.* When we fall into a difficult circumstance in which we cannot possibly do anything about it in an immediate sense, and we trust God to bring help in our life, it is okay to relax and find a good diversion as we ride along while we let God take over the wheel of our life.

Do not let a negative comment ruin your whole day, rather brush it off of the mind by acknowledging that no comment or criticism can ever define you. Do not let a harsh word play havoc in your head. Most people that you meet are driven by the ego, and as such are motivated by jealousy, greed, anger, pride, etc. Say something positive to those who criticize you, and even those who are mean to you. Thank them for giving you an opportunity to improve on yourself. Words of love can not only neutralize a negative emotion and bring about remorse on those acting on the negativity, but also cultivate humility in us and show our sincerity.

When you are criticized, do not jump into a conclusion that people are trying to pull you down. Oftentimes, we are being led by pride but we fail to recognize that in us. Pride is elusive in the self but shinning brightly on others. Try to find truth in a negative comment directed towards you. Pause and try to see a situation from other people's perspective, being impartial and with love. Do not let pride hinder you from accepting your shortcomings. We do not become lower by embracing our faults, much rather we become better. We all have rough edges which need polishing.

Prideful people can rarely learn from their mistake.

Remember that we are driven by what seems right to us, and sometimes what seems right to us is not necessarily right or true. The mind is limited in knowledge and it is easily swayed by opinions. Just look at the world of mass marketing. People are easily influenced even in the most personal matters. Opinions are personal views, and everyone has a bunch to offer. Moreover, the mind cannot separate truth from falsehood. The mind can know a fact, but it cannot "know" truth. The bottom line is that *We cannot totally rely on the mind*. However, this is not so with God because Godspace is omniscient and truth. As we walk in the Spirit, we derive our sense of self and confidence from the Self.

◊

Be willing to empathize with others. When we can relate to others, we are less prone to being led by pride. When we are able to feel happy for other's happiness, it becomes easier for us to find joy in our own life. When we are able to grieve for others, it does not add more grief onto us, but rather it brings us closer to the Spirit of

God. By doing good onto others we benefit ourselves as well, though we should not do good with any ulterior motive. In weeping with those who are weeping, we bring peace to the mourners and yet it also adds peace in our life. When we are clothed in humility, little things in life add colors onto us and thus our life becomes like a boldly colorful garden.

When we pray for others, we are not using up our heavenly brownie points or exhausting our "prayer account." If we feel unease or at loss when we pray for others, we need to recognize that we are being led by the ego which is inherently selfish. Praying by the carnal mind does not edify anyone. That kind of prayer only serves to boast the ego in looking pious and generous. A paper flower can add charm to our living-rooms, but on a closer look it is lifeless.

Without love a prayer is empty and dead.

Remember that you do not give anything away when you pray for someone in the Spirit, except for the time. However, time is insignificant to the Spirit. When we see the fruit of our prayer as people are benefited, our faith gets strengthened. Spiritual realm is quite opposite to that of the worldly physical realm. Whether it is joy, peace, or love, "sharing" it with others will not decrease it in us, but rather adds up more of it into our lives. Our sense of being increases as we embrace others spiritually. This is spiritual prosperity.

◊

When you are going through a difficult circumstance in life, do not try to see your life in all of its totality at once because you will only overwhelm yourself. When we are climbing a mountain and we feel exhausted as we walk uphill, looking towards the summit only makes us feel impatient and adds discouragement in us. Rather, we ought to take one step at a time in this journey of life by living one moment at a time. Besides, we cannot take more than one step at a time, we will stumble and fall trying!

At times circumstances in our life appear monstrous and crippling. Under such circumstances, we need to trust in God by acknowledging that God can help us through any circumstance because no circumstance is bigger than the Almighty God. When we move away from "I can handle it myself," or "I am helpless" attitude, and rely on God by trusting that if God were not able to help us then God would not have put us in such difficult situation, we start to experience a sense of ease and peace in life. Moreover, facing difficulties in life makes us stronger and mature. So, all in all, we come out better, stronger, and refined by going through the trials and tribulations in life.

◊

Try to develop self-control because that will save you from a lot of unnecessary headaches in life. Often we want things right now and without working for them. The carnal mind is prideful and even childish. It thinks that it can buy anything it wants or get it by throwing childish mental tantrum. However, things come to us in due time. We cannot get a harvest any sooner by pouring too much water on a plant; we may rather overwhelm the plant. In a religious sense people commit sin when they cannot wait for what they desire, and they take a "shortcut" to fulfill their want or need. For example, if we desire physical intimacy then we need to have patience to wait for the right person. Taking an abrupt step will only cause us pain and delay our objective in finding the right match or even cause us to lose an opportunity, though it may satiate the mind or the flesh momentarily.

Patience and self-control are synonymous.

◊

A Christian minister once told me that if there was one thing that the devil hates most in those who follow God then it is the godly people enjoying their life. Devil wants to see people worrying and in misery all the time. That is a good illustration to emphasize that the spiritual life does not have to be boring and painful. Living a spiritual life does not mean that we need to be living a life of suffering, struggle, or lack, although that does not mean that we cannot rejoice in such circumstances. We ought to do what we can to uplift our life (and usually we have an intuitive sense of that), and for everything else we need to give it (rely on) to God. Regardless of where we are, we can learn to live within our means, appreciate what we have, and take each moment at a time as we live our life fully and without any regret.

◊

No matter how difficult our life situation may get, we can find other people who are in worse situations. We only need to stop looking at ourselves through the magnifying glass of the ego, and look outward because the world is full of misery and suffering. Although it is callous to think like that, but if it helps us to console ourselves by giving us hope and motivates us in moving forward in life, then it is beneficial. Although we need to understand that it is walking in the gray area of apathy, which can morph into pride and in turn become fuel to the ego to further inflate one's false self.

The carnal mind is selfish by its innate nature, which is its survival mechanism. Humans have gone through many wars, famines, pestilences, and natural disasters, and through such conditions of scarcity the mind is "programmed" for its survival. Moreover, the mind constantly seeks comfort and safety. Yet for the mind these terms are relative. For example,

Some people twist and turn all night on a feathered bed, while there are those who sleep comfortably on a floor.

Some people are not happy unless it is a dinner with

steak, while there are those who are happy to get a regular meal.

Some people do not feel comfortable working for others or they constantly complain about their job, while there are those who feel fortunate to have a job.

Some people need all kinds of insurance in the world to feel secure, while there are those who feel safe with nothing.

Some people are not happy with their loving and faithful wife, while there are those who are desperately trying to find someone even to talk to.

Some people abuse their healthy body, while there are those who, despite lacking a body part, feel fortunate to be alive.

Shift your focus in life from *lack* to what you *have*. Often that makes a complete difference in our sense of happiness. We cannot be at two places at the same time, and similarly we cannot have our focus in the future (for something that is lacking in the present) and enjoy our life in the present (with something that is in the future). In other words, we need to count our blessings to experience happiness in life. Moreover, the mind can think of only one thing at a time. So if the mind is engaged in a thought of what we have then it is free from thinking about what we do not have. However, this requires us to actively goad the mind, especially when we are in a difficult situation.

◊

Try to find a bright spot in a situation you are in, no matter how gloomy it may seem to you. We will find a positive aspect if we try to cast our focus away from us and the negativity surrounding our situation. With patience and compassion for oneself, we are able to see the proverbial silver lining in the dark clouds of our situation. If nothing else, we will learn not to repeat the same mistake. Besides, we grow mature in the mind by facing life's difficulties. People who have not faced challenges in life are like little children, immature in their perspective of the world and blind to the Self.

If someone in your life leaves you, know that God has someone special for you who will appreciate you for who you are. *Do not let other people define you.*

If you lose a job, you can look for new opportunities or expand your career in a new field. *Do not let a job define you.*

Never think that your life is over because of one thing that went horribly wrong. If you blame yourself and ruminate on depressing thoughts, then those negative thoughts will attract even more and bigger negative thoughts, leaving you in a bad shape like a land ravaged by a hurricane. There are many things that can go wrong at this very moment, and thinking about them based on fear will be like playing a game under unfair rules. Even if something cannot be prevented from happening, our worrying will not do any good onto us. We need to remember that life goes on no matter what, and it is especially under the trying circumstances that we need to have faith in God because by ourselves we are no more than a little twig to a big hurricane.

◊

Improving The self

Be a rebel but do not be an extremist. When you are an extremist, you will be discouraged at every failure because life is not as perfect as we like to think about it. Seek positive change and do good.

Do not be led by any religious ideal, because they will make you feel guilty at every misstep or sin, and in turn will push you away from "God."

Be kind to yourself, and keep trying in your improvement.

Do not let your hope down.

Do not try to go from "zero to sixty" right away, you will only discourage yourself. Change happens over time as conditions become ready.

Do not give any room for pride over a success.

Try to be content with taking small baby steps. Often,

when our expectation is high, it becomes a hindrance.

Acknowledge God in your attempt to improve your habit so you are able to channel the strength in the Spirit. When the ego is denied, self-blame is denied as well, and all glory belongs to God.

Change is a nature of life. Even the mind is not as stable as we may like to think about it. Yes, when we are in our better days we feel encouraged and we end up achieving more, but then there are days when we feel low and discouraged. So when we do what we can without putting too much pressure on oneself and try to walk instead of run, then we will end up where we intend to go and find happiness in life as well. Taking it easy on ourselves is like a tortoise in the tale of a hare and a tortoise. Enjoy each step in the journey, and eventually we will reach our destination. Life is in the living, and those who hurry end up sooner to death.

◊

If your good is not good enough for others and that is only making you feel bad about yourself, it is time to explore new pasture. Never feel that your life will be incomplete without being with a certain person or in a group, or without working at a certain place. When our sense of being lies in the world, our happiness depends on other people or the world. The sad part about the ego is that it does not like to see others happy because it is inherently jealous. So with the world being the reflection of the ego, you will find many people who are quick to bring you down.

Remove the compulsive need in you to please others or to feel important in other's presence because often those attempts leave you feeling frustrated and empty. If you think or feel that you need to constantly offer something to a person to keep him or her with you or around you then that shows your insecurity, and in an extreme case it is an idolatry. When you put other people on a pedestal then you give them the ability to hurt you, and when you put yourself on a pedestal then you hurt yourself when you fall. Both are equally detrimental to you.

Be complete in yourself first, then you will truly appreciate other people for who they are. When desires, needs, judgment, or prejudice do not cloud our vision, we see other people beautiful in their soul. We are able to have a meaningful relationship with anyone when a relationship is not based on the expectations of the body or the mind. When we let the Spirit flow freely through us, we see relationships bloom because lasting relationships are spiritual in nature. The Spirit lacks nothing and it is the source of love, joy, and peace. Relationships based on sexual lust, allure of wealth, fame, or power lose their luster because the mind gets bored with a same thing after awhile, and beside looks, wealth, or fame cannot be sustained forever.

The flesh is only gratified momentarily, and like a natural predator that kills for fun and abandons its prey, the mind soon leaves what it has and craves for something else. The mind is never satisfied, and those who give into the mind are rarely happy. We forget to live our life in our pursuit for more. Our homes may be overstuffed, our garages may be filled, our mantelpiece crammed with rows of trophies, yet despite all the fame and fortune that the world offers, the ego is never satisfied, and consequently we are unhappy.

Giving into the ego is vanity.

To walk in love is to walk in the Spirit. Even if people are harsh to us, we can have compassion onto them because we see them helpless in the flesh as we find ourselves in. When we are able to take it easy in life and not act on the impulses of the ego, we have love onto oneself and others.

Love is the secret to happiness.

Well,

it is not a secret now after all.

Is

Life is full of suffering, accept it
acceptance is peace, do not resist it
resistance is misery, acknowledge it
pain is universal, don't hide from it

Surrender to God is freedom, try it
truth is empowering, stand on it
pride is blindness, drop it
humility is strength, adorn it

Love is power, embody it
giving is receiving, practice it
happiness is ephemeral, understand it
joy is within you, feel it

The world is vanity, don't cling to it

desire is infinite, free from it

fear is an illusion, see through it

courage is change, gird it

death is certainty, do not run from it

life is precious, pursue it

living is in this moment, experience it

God is within you, be enlightened.

8 FAITH

"Faith is the confidence in what we hope for and the assurance about what we do not see yet."
- Hebrews 11:1

We live by faith whether we acknowledge it or not. Faith is more than one's belief in a religion. For example, when we leave our home each morning to go to work or for an errand, we put our faith in a car to take us where we want to go without the car breaking down. When we get ready to sleep each night, we have faith that we will wake up the next morning. We even put our faith on an alarm clock. We have faith that each morning the sun will rise up and night will fall accordingly in due time. We put our faith in weather forecast, public services like police, fire department, traffic lights, etc. to function as they are supposed to. Indeed, we take most of these things for granted. But just imagine if the sun was not so reliable, our health was rather shaky, or our car was not so dependable. Now that would be a bumpy ride quite literally or otherwise. We live by putting our faith on things which we interact with daily.

Life without faith is filled with utter uncertainties, fear, and worries. When we look at our life, we do see uncertainties, fear, and worries, and there is no denying in that. *Complete freedom from uncertainties, fear, and worries is not possible to the mind because it is subjected to constant change, loss, or death.* However, we can have some degree of confidence, no matter how small, and that helps us to get by each day. Faith is the opposite of (or indirectly proportional to) uncertainties, fear, and worries in life. So the more faith we have on something, the less of the uncertainties, worries and fear associated with it. For example, if we had just bought a new car then our faith on the car would be strong and we would not have worry that it would break down on our way back from a dealer, whereas if we had bought a cheap jalopy then each little creaking noise while driving might give us a cringe.

For the carnal mind it is easy to put faith on things it can feel or experience with its senses. In other words, if we can measure something then we are more likely to put our faith on that thing, depending on whether the measurement meets our expectation. But that is not so with a spiritual matter. We cannot quantify love, hope, joy, peace, or faith. Often challenges in life push us to reach beyond the physical realm. That is why it is called a leap of faith, as one stops looking through the carnal eyes and starts looking through the spiritual eye, and makes the move despite all odds.

◊

Living in peace amidst storms in life needs strong faith, faith which is anchored in something stronger than oneself, other people, or even this world. It may seem rather cliché when someone says to believe in God or the Higher power. But to have a strong faith in God entails our surrender, which in turn requires humility. The natural mind will not give an inch to anyone or anything unless it needs something in return or when it is shown its vulnerability. In other words, pride will never surrender to God, unless it is brought very low. Hence those who have gone through the bitter trials and tribulations in life have the opportunity to have strong faith in God as the defense system of the ego is ruptured by the continuous cycle of suffering and helplessness in the flesh. Inside suffering is the seed of transcendence to the higher spiritual consciousness.

Suffering does not necessarily result in spiritual awakening or spiritual edification. Otherwise people suffering in war or poverty stricken regions in the world will be spiritually awakened automatically. However, most people in such circumstances are scarred by mental agony and fear. Spiritual awakening happens by the grace of God. People can hit their rock bottom and call it a quit on life, or continue to live in denial according to the carnal mind. Suffering is never pleasant, but suffering is brought about by the nature of the carnal mind, which is also reflected in the world. If we accept life no matter what and surrender ourselves to God then that opens up our willingness to be led by the Spirit. When the mind is under the Spirit, we have freedom, peace, and joy.

Meditation Practice

We can try to be attuned to the Spirit by practicing sitting quietly and watching the mind. The mind likes to keep the sense of control by constantly grasping at any thought in Godspace, or by giving into the needs and desires of the body. Meditation helps us in separating our soul from the mind and the body. It is amazing how much chatter goes on in our head constantly. We can focus on breath as we breathe in and out deeply and consciously. Breath is happening in real-time or the present moment, so when we are aware of breathing, we are aware of the present moment. Be like a surfer riding a big wave who is very aware of the wave underneath.

If you find yourself frustrated by the unfocused and distracted mind, practice by saying (not verbally, just in the mind) long "A" as you breathe in, followed by long "B" as you breathe out, and then long "B" as you breathe in, followed by long "A" as you breathe out. The mind likes simplicity and order, for example A -> B -> C -> D, or A -> B, A -> B. The abrupt pattern of A -> B, B -> A which changes in each breath helps to hold the mind from wandering off. The objective of this breathing meditation is to touch the source of all life which is within us but just beyond the mind. Through meditation we can experience the oneness in the Spirit.

◊

Sometimes we hear a saying, "Be spiritual, but not religious." Saying like this is popular because of all the divisions and conflicts in the world in the name of religion. Religion by itself is not good or bad. It can be a noble tool to direct us in our journey home. However, when people are led by wrong ideologies and resort to violence to accomplish their motive, then we see the ills that are evident in the world. Most, if not all religions, are centered on love, though many have morphed into a completely different form due to religious adultery. That is why we need to be on guard, and be selective in filtering truth within a religion. Seek to find the spiritual pearl in the sea which is wide and wild. When our spiritual eye is open, we do not feel compelled to label ourselves with any religious badge, nor do we feel encumbered by the bondage of legalism.

◊

Faith is a personal experience whether it is in a

common sense or in a religious context. Even within a church, faith is that of each individual congregant. There is "faith in a church," but there is no "faith of a church." A church or sangha can provide a loving and inviting environment to foster faith of its members. *Where there is love, the Spirit prospers*. Yet it is not the Spirit that is prospering because the Spirit is already perfect. We prosper when the Holy Spirit is revealed more and more in us. The Spirit is like the *"flavor in salt."*

Usually faith grows gradually. It is like a tree that starts with a small seed and grows tall and strong to bear much abundant fruit. It takes circumstances in life that are bigger than us to move our faith to a new height. Like a budding tree that grows more with rainfall, so does our faith in adversities. The mind becomes comfortable when everything seems normal to the point where it feels self-sufficient. In other words, ease and comfort in life has the potential to drive us away from God. When we stop depending on our finite self, and the "security" of the world, and seek the One who is the master of all laws in the Universe, we give the way to a new road paved by faith in yet unknown but true indeed.

◊

We should not have the attitude of a needy child when it comes to faith. When we were children, we might had the confidence that what we ask of our parents for Christmas or our birthday, we would receive that thing. God is not a Santa Claus, so we need to remove that mental concept because that will only alienate us from God. Sometimes things work out our way, and other times things fail. Especially when things fall apart in our life that we are inclined to base our faith on the fulfillment of our expectations or prayers. Disappointments under trying times can push us further away from God. We need to understand that things fall in place in our life when we are karmically ready for them, not a moment sooner nor a moment later.

Having said that, we need to have faith like that of a little child. We need to have confidence that what we ask for will be provided for. If we do not have faith then why even pray, because without faith a prayer is like a wishful thinking. Yet, we need to understand that faith goes hand in hand with our willingness to walk in the will of God. Moreover, in order for us to be blessed we need to be karmically ready for the things we ask for. That is why it is important that we do good no matter what, so we are always under God's favor (so to speak).

If we look from the Spiritual perspective, our soul lacks nothing because the Spirit that sustains us is perfect and all encompassing. When we walk in the Spirit, we do not see things selfishly as mine. Yet we are in this physical body, and we are, in a sense, separated from the rest. However, when we put others first and walk in love, then good things generally fall in our life. This is a miracle of walking in love that we are blessed by God, and all in all God is just.

◊

You have faith or you don't. In other words, faith is an absolute term. There is no gray area in faith. Faith can be small and growing. So it is wrong to say, "I have ninety percent faith in that." That way of thinking is affected with the lack of our confidence. Faith dispels doubts in us.

"Him who lacks (wisdom), let him ask of God, who gives to all liberally and without reproach, and it will be given to him. But let him ask in faith, with no doubting. For he who doubts is like a wave of the sea driven and tossed by the wind. For let not that man suppose that he will receive anything from the Lord; he is a double minded man, unstable in his ways. "

- James 1:5- 7

The mind always seeks the sense of security, and faith is the cure for our fear and insecurity in life. While we can never have the absolute sense of security in the mind, yet we can have enough sense of security in the Spirit, which makes night and day difference in our life. When we have faith in God, we are at peace knowing that if it is not in God's will then no grave ill can befall on us, and if we do stumble and fall in life then God's arm is right over us to help us get back up again.

Just as a baby starts to crawl before it learns to walk, for our faith to flourish we need to see our faith work in smaller things in our life. Opportunities will present themselves to us when we are ready. Faith is like a journey in itself, as we reach new heights we see more and bigger works of faith, and finally our soul becomes like intertwined with the Spirit, and we see the universe simply unfolding, like flowers opening up to the sunshine. Seen through our spiritual eye, we see miracles happening all around. Life is a miracle in itself.

The carnal mind separates us from our true Self. We need to discipline the mind by acknowledging the presence of God within us. By this mind alone, it is very limited and can only do what it has already learned. It is not much different from a computer in terms of its functionality. It is only through Godspace that we intuitively know and are able to push new frontiers. As we rely more on God, our faith grows correspondingly, and consequently the ego is humbled.

◊

Our faith can ebb, so it needs a constant pouring of the spiritual oil to keep the lamp of faith burning. No one among us is immune to that, and especially with all the temptations in the world, it is easy to fall back into the ways of the flesh. We continue to walk in faith by trusting in God no matter what, and by appreciating all the blessings in our life. If we are spiritually sound, and if things do not work out according to our expectation, then we can have peace knowing that failures in life do not corresponds to God's love for us. *Sometimes good things are not pleasant to the mind, and other times pleasant things are not good for us.* A baby feels good in the warmth of its pee, but when it gets cold and uncomfortable, it starts to cry. In life we crave for things that are not good for us, and we even grieve over such things if God prevents us from having such things. With the spiritual wisdom comes the realization that what we need God provides, and everything else is vanity.

Rather than asking, "What's in it for me?" we need to ask, "What's in it for others?" When we bless others any way we can, our blessing from God is added onto us and it never runs dry. Just as God is infinite, blessing from God is unlimited. It is the mind which thinks in terms of scarcity as it dwells in poverty.

"Give, and it will be given to you; good measure, pressed down, shaken together, and running over will be put into your bosom ."

- Luke 6:38

◊

The carnal mind likes to sit in the throne adorned with pride and declare limitations on things that it has basically no control over. When we are led by the carnal mind, we even suspect about the things that God can do in our life. *The ego secretly thinks that it is God.* Torn between the Spirit and the ego is our soul. We are born in this physical world, and as such we have the natural affinity to be identified with the mind. It is only when we are born again (in the Spirit) that we become aware of our true Self. The ego tries to box the spiritual into the physical, and consequently we are robbed from seeing the miracles in our life and experiencing our perfection in the Spirit.

◊

Looking From The Karmic Perspective

Faith in God is needed when we fall into difficult times in life. The carnal mind will give up when it is pushed far enough. However, the limitation of the mind is an opportunity for the Spirit, which has been shrouded by the darkness of the ego, to be finally revealed unrestricted. However, that does not usually happen because most people are not ready for the revelation of the God essence in them. Whether it is a karmic propensity or otherwise is a matter of discussion in itself, yet it is logical to view from the perspective of karma.

Why is one person saved in an accident, while others die in the same accident?

Why is one child born with a disability, while its siblings are born without any disability?

What made you to be born in the family you were born in and not in another family in some other part of the world?

These are some of the difficult questions that defy human knowledge and wisdom. We can try to answer these questions with mathematical probabilities or through

DNA analysis, but we still find ourselves short to answer these types of question, especially when they relate to our soul. Furthermore, we can accept these facts as the will of God, and that will not be wrong either. However, God is omniscient and knows every hair on our head.

Our actions, no matter how small or insignificant to us, have consequences. Just like our good deeds harbor heavenly treasure (good karma), our bad deeds incur bad fruits (bad karma). A soul is eternal, but manifests in the physical realm according to its karmic proclivity. We reap what we sow, and the physical realm is no limitation to the spiritual essence. Just like a goldsmith heats rough gold in a fiery furnace and hammers it until it is a fine jewelry, a soul is refined into perfection being subjected to this fallen world until it is finally illuminated in the Spirit.

Rare are those who cross to the other shore, and rare also are those who attempt to cross the divide. So if you are on the path, take heart, for countless souls are asleep in the world.

◊

Faith in God requires the surrender of our personal will, which in turn requires humility in us. Faith in God also leads us to walk in love. Yet it is through the grace of God that we are spiritually awakened. Apart from God's will, what is? Now God is not a human to view something as good or bad, because God incorporates everything. From God's perspective everything is. Evil is the absence of good, just like darkness is the absence of light. It is through the mind that we define good or evil. Everything in the creation is climbing the ladder of Godspace. If one being appears anti-life then that is struggling at the lower realm of Godspace. Everything is a part of Godspace because apart from God there is nothing.

Ultimately the faith to finally transcend this physical realm to God Consciousness comes from knowing who we are in the Spirit. In a spiritual sense, when we "know", we "become." This is different from our mental concept of knowing. For example, we can say that we know how a victim of a tsunami felt, but to really "know" how a tsunami victim felt, we have gone through the pain of the natural disaster. That is why it is rather amiss to say, "I know God" when we "think" that we know God.

◊

Faith in God is needed to avoid paranoia in our life. If we listen to the news, it may make us feel uneasy with the amount of bad things happening in the world. There are uncertainties with regards to the economy, breakdown of the society, natural disasters, terrorism, war, famine, wide spread of infectious disease, etc. All of these scenarios, whether probable or otherwise, can make us feel helpless because these problems are bigger than us individually. We feel that we cannot do anything to change even a little bit. So the sense of paranoia starts to settle into our psyche and consequently the thoughts in our head, words, and actions are negatively affected. Some people start building bunkers, others start buying gold and silver, stocking on nonperishable food, and what not. While those who have the means can prepare for the predicted doom (though their fear is right behind them), but what about the rest of the population who are left alarmed? The sense of uncertainties and helplessness under fear can seriously affect our daily life.

We can give all uncertainties to God and lighten the unnecessary burden off of our back by relying on God with the faith that God can and will lead us and protect us. The Almighty God has the ultimate say in any situation. Oftentimes, we see miracles under extraordinary circumstances. What is too big for us individually as well as as a society is not big enough for God. *In other words, there is nothing too big or too small for God to handle*. When we feel disheartened by what we hear in the news, we can have peace knowing that God is in control after all. Besides, what is meant to be will happen anyways. We need to have our hope in the spiritual life and not so much in this earthly life which can end anytime. When we are grounded in the Spirit, we are free from the unnecessary worries and fears of the mind. Consequently, we find ourselves happy.

Ups and Downs in Faith

I said to myself, "I will love everyone, and I will even take
other's pain."
I felt I understood the will for my life, I was full of zeal.

I happen to walk down a busy street, and saw people
oppressing those less fortunate than them.
It was unfair and unjust, "why can't they feel other's
pain?"

Then I wondered, "what's the point?" For those being
oppressed were once oppressing others,
mercy was not in either heart, they were blindly adding
more tears.

I saw the wheel of Samsara turning before these very
eyes,
on and on it went, crushing dreams and happiness of

those under.

*Then I realized that the world has been the same all
along, just new actors and the set
the strings are the same, and the one pulling them the
same also.*

*I felt distanced and indifferent. Indeed, this is a tragedy.
"you are strong, you are wise, O man, but you are blind."*

*I felt this life all vain, I cannot possibly change anything!
I even questioned my own existence, for everything
seemed meaningless.*

*then it occurred to me that I was being driven by the
same wind
that my faith was shaken by the ways of the world.*

*"Look! the one who tried to change the world."
they killed some, and some just lost their heart.*

*yet despite all that, light is never overcome by the
darkness
and hope clings onto few who dare to walk against the
wind.*

*I saw that in darkness everyone falls,
those being oppressed and those oppressing others.*

with the heavy heart, I prayed for them all
for I saw that the one who is oppressing needed it the
most.

evil is a vicious cycle, love is the only answer
forgiveness to all is the way to our freedom.

⑨ LETTING GO

It is not so much as we own possessions in this world, but the world through the possessions that owns us.

Whether when you feel that your life is filled with vanity and that there is nothing meaningful in all your desires and wants, or when you are lost in the endless cycle of cravings without a sense of lasting satisfaction, you need to free yourself from the compulsive and possessive nature of the carnal mind. The carnal mind constantly tries to make anything as its because that is how it fuels its sense of aliveness. For the carnal mind to be still or quiet is synonymous to its dying, and hence it is rather terrifying for the mind to wake up in the middle of one night (or day) and experience the utter emptiness of life. We feel that emptiness in varying degree at some point in our life. Most of the time we revert back to our "normal" routine, and we try to numb that "pain" or void feeling with any distraction we can find. TV, music, video games, books, sports, shopping, food, drinks, drugs, sex, or even our family or church can be our avenue of that temporary relief or escape. Yes if we long for the Sunday morning in a church to feel "alive," but otherwise our life is just mundane or "normal," then sadly the church hour is our weekly "fix."

If we try to fill a sinkhole in our backyard with more air or water, the hole will still be wide open and continue to stare back at us. You will think that it is rather nonsensical to cover that sinkhole with a big tarp either. You may say, *"But the sinkhole is still there, see! I, or someone I love, might fall into that big hole."* You do not want a big sinkhole in your backyard, nor anywhere remotely near your house. A BIG no-no. Yet we so naively tolerate sinkholes in our psyche, whether in ignorance or otherwise. That "sinkhole" in us is the spiritual void or the spiritual longing of our soul.

Let's face it, we are all lost in this world, some are more lost than others, and many do not even know that they are lost and are "happy" in this world of illusions. The mind does not know where it is going. The mind does not even want to acknowledge that death is waiting for it. So in its attempt to be complete, the mind tries to occupy itself with different things or people. Those avenues help us to forget about the pain and the hollowness in our life, but only temporarily. On the one hand, we do not want to feel the emptiness of life, and on the other hand, the mind does not have any other way to solve this spiritual crisis. So we get caught up being addicted on other people or things. However, no substance or person can ever take the place of God, who gives our soul its true identity. An addiction is not a problem in itself, but rather is a sign or a symptom pointing to the spiritual hunger within us. The spiritual void is the longing for our spiritual home, which is our destination.

We need to understand that just because people say that they do not believe in God does not negate the spiritual dimension in them. People can live in denial or ignorance all their life, but when that spiritual void stares at them squarely at some point in their life, the feeling of desperation and pain will be the same regardless. Truth can be hidden but it cannot be made a lie, and just because we believe a truth as a lie does not make it a lie. We are in this physical body, but our essence is spiritual. Yet by ourselves we cannot transcend the gap from physical to spiritual. It is only through the grace of God that we are able to be free from this *samsara* .

◊

The cure for the inner discontent in us is spiritual in nature, and it is rather paradoxical to say that the antidote for the "void" in us is to "letting go" of the things that are tying us down in this world. Iron shackles and bars are not the only form of things that restrict our freedom. Any worldly possession or relationship can be that impediment to our soul. When we stop in vain to add more of the worldly goods into our life, we give an opportunity for the Spirit of God to be revealed in us. It is like the wind that drives clouds to reveal the sun. So when it comes to the worldly things in our life, it is an apt saying, "Less is more." The more we have, the more that takes up our time and our attention, the more there is to lose, and the more there is to worry about.

We need to stop thinking that we are the master of our life. Thought pattern like, "I need to do this in order to survive" may seem empowering to the ego, but it separates us from God. Things that will happen in our life will happen regardless. Trials and tribulations are a part of our life. We are given free will, but we, as the mind, cannot change our destiny. Like an apple that falls down to the ground due to gravity, the carnal mind is influenced by selfishness, pride, jealousy, greed, etc. This is not meant to vilify the mind. The mind is helpless because it acts according to the needs and desires of the body, and from what it has already learned but not forgotten.

It is only when a drowning person stops struggling frantically and lets a lifeguard rescue him or her that the person can be saved. We need to have a humble acknowledgment that God is in control. Just because something does not go according to our expectation does not negate God. The very thought that comes to the mind is by the will of God. God encompasses everything in the creation. As we give more to God, we experience more freedom. There is nothing to add nor anything to lose in the Spirit. *The Spirit of God is always perfect.* The moment we absolutely realize that God got us no matter what, is the point in our life where our faith in God is perfected. When we know in our soul that we are a part of God and the Spirit is within us, we are enlightened.

◊

Now this may seem rather counter-intuitive when we are told to focus on our hurt in order to letting go of it, but that's what is needed to overcome any negative emotion in us. This is different from thinking or worrying about a hurt, which rather than helping us, add more fuel to the fire. Dwelling on our past hurt is like a cow regurgitating and chewing its cod. When we let the light of Godspace, which is the spiritual awareness, be shed on a hurtful emotion then we let the power of God to overcome the darkness in us.

"Be still and know that I am God."
- Psalm 46:10

Sit quietly, and be aware of the body, the mind, thought, and any hurtful emotion in the mind.

Let go of all things that are pulling you down. In this present moment, simply be like a leaf floating on a river.

Breathe deeply and feel your breath, relax.

Focus on any emotional hurt in you, or invite a negative emotion in the mind to surface.

Remember that it is not the mind but the Spirit doing the healing. When you are attuned to the source of life, you become one with the Spirit.

Be impartial, no judgment, and if tears come because you are deeply hurt then let it flow, but know that God is in control after all. Remember that God's love for you in unconditional. Feel God's love in each breath you take.

Let the power of God heal you as you sit still.

Feel the peace of God settle in you. If you feel bothered then pray onto God and give your burden onto God.

This meditation can be practiced in a group with someone more spiritually mature. Be open, however, and if you are comfortable, talk to someone you trust. There is a spiritual synergy in a loving sangha which promotes spiritual growth and healing.

◊

Let your mind be like a pan coated with Teflon, which neither lets oil nor water sticks on to it. Do not hold onto any comment, good or bad. A good comment makes us feel good momentarily, and a bad one makes us feel miserable. Yet both are playing with the mind. Imagine yourself in a movie theater, and picture the mind moving from one scene onto the next in the movie. If we dwell on one scene then that will ruin the whole movie for us. To be spiritually free, we need to rise above what others think or say of us. The mind is influenced by other's opinions, but the Spirit is steadfast because it is the truth and always free.

We need to let go of the need to feel important because we cannot always be important to others or the world. The world of fame is like the game of Musical Chairs, in which someone always loses because the one playing the music has abundant subjects. Besides, what goes up eventually must come down. When we do not exalt ourselves on praises, we become less vulnerable to being driven by pride. This is because when we feed into pride, it will become hungry again like a little pet. Pride is the cause of much of our problems in life. We prop up our self-image so high that it needs constant supply of egoic fuel to keep it flying high. Isn't it easy to land that self-advertising blimp, and start living our life unburdened by what other people think or say about us? Indeed it is, but the carnal mind is infatuated with the egoic gratification, and that is why those who are led by the ego are unhappy.

When we acknowledge that we are a soul, then we are able to be unaffected by praises or criticisms of others. Other's opinions matter to the mind but not to a soul. Nothing that others say about us can take away our true identity in the Spirit or our relationship with God. This is also the freedom from unnecessary self-inflicting tendencies found in most of us. We are concerned about looks, body, job, house, car, etc. and we let those things define us. Let all such thoughts and feelings pass off of you. Worldly things like looks, body, job, relationship, or money are not permanent, and to base our foundation of our identity on such things is like building a house on sand. Be at peace from the unwanted burdens by internalizing your soul identity in the Spirit. Besides, life on earth is too short to live in constant fear and worries associated with the carnal mind.

◊

There are some days when we feel just exhausted, physically and/or emotionally. Do not force yourself to do anything your heart is not into; otherwise you will spend far more time, energy, or other resources, and in turn you will fail to find much fulfillment in that. Do not hesitate to take a nap, meditate, go for a walk in nature, or do something that is relaxing and edifying to the soul. However, do not engage in anything that promotes violence, lie, or is morally wrong. Things that serve the flesh will push us further away from the Spirit of God.

When the Bible talks about taking a weekly Sabbath, it is for our own benefit and not for God. If God were to take rest then everything will cease. Body, mind, and soul need regular rest. It is apparent that the body and the mind need regular rest, but one may wonder how does a soul rests! When we sleep, the body and the mind are resting. Especially when a sleep is without a dream, then the mind is able to rest unobstructed. Under sleep the mind is not as active in defending its false sense of self or the ego. This gives a soul an opportunity to connect to Godspace. The soul longs for the true Sabbath which is the rest in the eternal home or its perfection in the Spirit. When the soul is able to connect to Godspace, it is at rest. Beside sleep, a soul can find that rest in meditation.

◊

Difficult situation in life is a cue from God that we need a change in life. It can be relocation, loss of job, loss of a relationship or friendship, illness, or sudden change in our life event. Often we become comfortable in life and start living in the flesh and distancing ourselves from the Spirit. Being comfortable in the world is an impediment to a soul. However, suffering in life does not automatically elevate us spiritually. Oftentimes, we find a substitute for a thing lost, and we continue with our life like before, which is basically the carnal mind cheating us of an opportunity to seek the perfect substitution for all of our longings in life, which is the Spirit of God.

Change is seldom pleasant to the mind, but change is a way of life. We can try to run away from it, hide from it (deny), or accept it. If we try to run away from unpleasant circumstances in life then we really do not rid ourselves of them. Those circumstances will be nearby closing in on us. So we end up living in constant fear and worry. If we try to deny what is real and live our life lying to ourselves then that will not make what is real a fantasy. We will eventually have to swallow the bitter pill and accept what is our reality or continue to live in denial. Living in denial is not life. However, if we accept an unfortunate episode in our life then it will be unpleasant for awhile, but we will eventually overcome it. We end up learning from our struggles, becoming more mature, strong, and being able to effectively face similar situations in life. So, all in all, it is for our own good that we face the difficult situations in life head on.

◊

Do not let your job, family, friends, or the society change you. Do not change yourself to fit in, either. You can be comfortable in your skin, and still be a productive member of a society. Let go of any compulsive desire or "need" in you to feel important or be somebody. Be nobody to the world, and then you will be at peace, because you will be free from all expectations, whether it is your own or of others. When there is nothing to prove and "no-one" to be, we are not bothered by the cares of the world. Those who try to prove to be somebody to the world keep trying to prop up the ego, and often in vain. The ego is a bottomless pit, and trying to please the ego is a never ending quest. Happiness is natural when we are complete in ourselves.

Simple Meditation

Breathe in deeply, and say to yourself,

"I am complete in the Spirit ."

As you breathe in, feel the presence of the Holy Spirit within you.

Breathe out deeply, and say to yourself,

"I am free from all expectations, and there is nothing for me to prove ."

As you breathe out, feel the freedom in the Spirit.

Do this several times as meditation. This brings about a sense of completeness and peace in us.

◊

Try not to dwell on hurt or what brings you down emotionally. If something has already happened and you cannot change it, accept it and move on. For example, a person who is divorced becomes a Christian. The person reads in the scripture that divorce for trivial reason is a sin, and he or she is then convicted in heart for the divorce. We cannot just pretend that something did not happen in our life because we do not like it or approve of it now! Many people live in denial, and do anything to hide an unpleasant truth from others or even from themselves. But the nature of a lie is that it is like mire. A lie leads to more lies and people go deeper in that spiritual mire. It is easier to just let go of the need to prove that we are perfect or even decent. A mistake does not define us, but a lie can paint a wrong picture about us.

Telling a truth is always better. Truth sets us free from a burden that a lie, otherwise, exerts. There is no fear, guilt, or remorse associated with a truth because they are of the carnal mind. When we take courage to tell the truth, the darkness associated with a lie loses its stronghold over us. Never assume that something that seems acutely absurd to us will be interpreted the same way by others. Oftentimes, people are accepting or at least not harsh if we tell the truth. We are often unfair to ourselves as we look at us through the magnifying glass of the ego.

So you made a mistake or something is wrong with you; what is the worst that can happen to you if you tell the truth?

People will talk about you? Slander you?

People will laugh at you?

People will not take you seriously?

People will "unfriend" you?

Well, that is not so bad after all, is it? If you analyze the above questions, you will recognize the needs of the ego. The ego wants to feel important, and it wants to exert its control over others. When we try to disidentify from the ego and identify with the Spirit, we are free from the compulsive nature of the ego which is possessive and controlling. In other words, we do not have to worry about what others think or say about us. Will you rather be free or live a lie? Now it will be naive and foolish to confess our wrong onto everyone we meet. The world is governed by the ego. In general, it is better for people whom we come across regularly to know things about us which are, otherwise, an open secret. Having said that, we need to use prudence and sound discernment.

◊

"What do you really need in life?"

Here are few things as mentioned by real people in a popular dating website as the things they cannot live without; namely air, water, food, church, family, friends, money, pet, car, phone, computer, sex, weed, music, etc. Those are a mix of things as presented by few people diverse in ethnicity, age, race, or social strata. Now some of these things like pet, church, weed, for instance, seem like we can live without, but what about many other things that are part of our life, which we are intimately attached to? Have you given any thought about them? Relationships end, things break, and people die. We really do not have any control over them. Sure we can be responsible and delay the inevitable, but if we childishly cling onto them then that brings about sorrow in us.

When we base our sense of life and happiness on things, people, or anything outside of us then eventually we will end up being unhappy when those things do not work or when people leave us. Moreover, we should refrain from deriving our sense of happiness from our body, looks, race, intelligence, etc. We cannot expect the wind to blow in one direction all the time, and when things go against our expectations, we become sad. To be above all worldly appeals, is the safeguard for our soul. This is the principle of *non-attachment* that the Buddha talked about. Non-attachment does not mean that we become like robots, and indifferent to other people around us and their lives. We have our relationships, we love others, we empathize with others, help others, we use resources to fulfill the needs of our body, and we enjoy our life, but we are free from them and there is no clinginess with others or the world. In other words, we are in the world but not attached to the world (or of the world).

We experience the spiritual freedom when we are able to love others. There is no clinginess in true love because love is in the selfless act of devotion. Love is unconditional and non-attachment. In love, there is no expectation, desire, or need. In love, we are able to rejoice in other's happiness, and mourn in their sorrow. In love, we do not try to possess others nor control them. We set them free, just as we are free.

To love is to be.

◊

We should take the worldly possession in life as our

blessings from God. That way we do not end up idolizing material things in life. As a good steward, we should use our blessings while enjoying our life. We should not invest our sentimental values on the material objects or people. Although most people in the west are materialistic, they do not worry too much if their toaster, TV, or washing machine were to break when compared to people in poor countries. This is because well off people quickly replace a broken gadget with a new one. The point here is that even without realizing, most people, who are otherwise materialistic, do not get attached to ordinary things. Misdirected emotional attachments bring about unnecessary headache in life to us because things break, get old, or stolen. To be free from the pain of separation, loss, or loneliness, we need to free ourselves from all emotional attachments in life.

Worldly people are in constant fear of losing something that they have or hold dear. It is like a tale of a rich man who sleeps (if he can get any) on a mattress stuffed with gold for fear that his wealth will be stolen. This is a sad malady of the worldly possessions, they end up possessing us instead. For a rich person, letting go of wealth is not an easy feat. It is like losing one's identity. That is why Jesus said that it is easier for a camel to enter through the eye of a needle than for a rich man to enter the kingdom of heaven. Yet, with practice it is not impossible. If you have a hard time tithing, giving donation for a good cause, or doing something good for others selflessly, then start with a little amount or a small act of kindness. Acknowledge that everything is of God anyway. For many of us it is an uphill battle to go against the selfish and possessive nature of the carnal mind. Yet no good deed is insignificant. When we see people benefiting and our actions are making positive impact in people's lives, we feel a sense of joy in our soul. That joy brings about positive motivation in us to become more loving and more giving.

Love *always* *wins* .

So,

Start somewhere, anywhere.

Unburden yourself by letting go of all the emotional attachments to this world and everything it offers.

Be generous, be giving, and you will be blessed.

Set your mind on the spiritual things, and try to see through the spiritual eye.

Spiritual Fruit

Material blessings are not all that there is. Joy and peace are more precious blessings to have.

Kings long to conquer the spiritual fruit, but they can not possess it with all their might.

Wise men attempt to discern it, but they can not understand it with all their wisdom.

Rich men seek to buy it, but they can not acquire it with all their wealth.

Yet a poor monk has it, a pilgrim finds it, and a child radiates with it.

Soul Calling

I heard a calling in the dark; I looked around, no one to
be found
Sinful nature had left on this heart its mark; I was proud,
bound to fall to the ground.

I gave into every desire; was not compelled to anything
holy, was at the mercy of the evil
I was happy in the mire; felt strong in my folly, was of no
good avail.

My eyes were shrouded; I stumbled, took a big fall
My soul was wounded; I trembled, finally hit the wall.

I was desperate; I felt lonely, like a fawn lost from its doe
I blamed my fate; I cried vehemently, felt helpless with
nothing I could do.

I heard a calling in the dark; I looked around, no one to be found
Sinful nature had left on this heart its mark; I was proud, bound to fall to the ground.

I closed my eyes; prayed to the Lord, poured out my soul
I felt the Spirit rise; as I longed to hear the Word, in loving arms to be hold.

I felt peace despite the trial; there was nothing more to lose, nothing to fear
I was at ease despite the wail ; in humility there was no ruse, no vanity nor care.

Joy was bubbling within me; being under His grace, a new life blessed with
My heart sings praises in me; being in His warm embrace, with my soul uplift.

10 SURRENDER

Love (of God) sets us free

The word "surrender" connotes negative feeling or emotion with its dark, fearful, helpless, and giving up implications. The carnal mind does not like to think that it is inferior to anything or anybody, nor does it like to give away an inch of its turf. It likes to continue sitting on the pedestal of vanity. Pride is the hallmark of the carnal mind, and it will do anything to keep the sense of being important or in control. That is why the carnal mind constantly seeks attention or praise. Even in suffering or a difficult situation, the carnal mind seeks the secret attention, the feeling of being in the limelight. So, whether it is a sunny day or a rainy day, it is never a wasteful day for the carnal mind.

A worldly person is under the bondage of the carnal mind. We just need to look around to see how people bring pain and suffering onto themselves and others by acting according to the carnal mind. This is because the carnal mind is limited in its capability and knowledge, and it is vulnerable to the needs and desires of the flesh. The carnal mind cannot solve a problem when the problem is itself. Hence we need power greater and beyond the mind to transcend the mind. The Spirit which gives us life is our guide and the source of power in our journey to the perfection of the soul.

◊

Surrender, here, is the surrendering of our false sense of "I," which is the ego, to God. When we empty ourselves, we let the Spirit of God to move in (figuratively speaking). The new "I," which identifies with the Spirit, is humble and does not need to defend itself constantly nor has the undue needs or desires of the egoic "I." The mind under the Spirit is free from the inner mental noise because it does not have fear, constant cravings, or cares of the world. This state of being is the spiritual freedom, and the person who is free has peace and joy. In it is the oneness with the Spirit.

Surrender is the humility towards God. When we truly acknowledge that everything that we are and everything that we have is from God, we cannot help but be humble before God. This humility is like that of a child towards its parents. A child is dependent on its parents or primary caregiver for even basic functions. Our relationship with God should be personal and primary, otherwise if the ego takes the control, "I" is far from God.

Even though we cannot sense God with the mind or the five senses, God is always with us. It is we who are usually away from God. When we are attuned to Godspace, we are like a leaf that has fallen in a river that flows by the current of water. As such there is no boasting in being in oneness with the Spirit of God. There is nothing to say like, "I did this," "I am this," or "I am that." We are a vessel for the Spirit, and we become like a vehicle for "I Am" to fulfill the will of God.

As we grow in the Spirit, our faith becomes stronger, and consequently we become sure of the voice that has always been within us. This is the intuition in the Spirit. The Spirit is our guide, sustainer, and everything as we find our identity in God. A religion can point us in our journey, but it is the Spirit that moves us. So we have to go beyond a religion to find the oneness in the Spirit. If we draw a line and say, "God is this" and settle for that, then that will be our threshold, but not of God. God is Omnipotent, Omnipresent, and Omniscient, and, besides, who has measured God?

◊

Surrender to God is neither pessimism nor a sign of our weakness. The world gives us a false sense of identity in form which desires attention, whereas the Spirit of

God gives our soul its true identity, which is perfect in every aspect. When we surrender ourselves to God, we are not giving up or giving away anything real, but at the same time we are unburdening ourselves. What is false cannot be accounted for, and what has always been there, can be hidden but cannot be unaccounted for. The ego or the carnal mind is false, but the Spirit is the truth. *To surrender ourselves to God is to gain oneself*. So to lose the egoic "I" is to gain the real "I," and this is a divine paradox.

◊

"This is mine," says the mind.

The mind likes to play the game of Monopoly in real life. On a broad scale, the world is a reflection of an individual ego. That is a sad aspect of the world we live in where people become selfish and "mechanical." Yet the Spirit within us wants to love everyone unconditionally. However, under the bondage of the carnal mind, a person cannot help to yield to the Spirit. This is like a crowd mentality where an individual is influenced by the mass. Each one of us is like a transceiver (a technical term for a device which is a transmitter as well as and a receiver) to Godspace. We are affected by the collective level of Consciousness around us. With the majority of the world in the spiritual darkness, samsara feeds and fuels itself.

The carnal mind wants to acquire and possess

whether it is worldly object or people. It is not concerned about the well being of others. However, the nature of Godspace is such that we are all connected in our innermost being. So when a part of the population is suffering, that affects the whole population spiritually. This is reflected in a country where a dictator rules with iron grip with few other elites while the rest of the population live in a squalid condition. The overall spiritual state of such country is dim. Those who are ruled are subjected to fear and poverty, while those who rule are ruled by the carnal mind. It is a misery to be lost in *samsara*.

◊

We do what seems good to us regardless of our cultural, economic, educational, or religious background. When we are being led by the carnal mind, we do what appeals to the mind which is often not the best thing for us or others. This is because the carnal mind is limited, and led by pride, needs, and desires of the flesh. Like a moth that is attracted to flame, one who is led by the carnal mind often gets burned. Whereas when we are led by the Spirit, truth appeals onto us. In a sense, we become truth.

Our soul longs for the spiritual rest in God. A soul seeks to be perfected in the Spirit. We are a part of God, and our soul (us) wants to be in the holy union. Whenever the mind pushes us away from God, we feel bad in our innermost being. Have you felt bad when you lied? That is our soul grieving. Anytime we are led astray by the carnal mind, the Spirit convicts us. If we continue to ignore the Spirit calling then we become callous and let the carnal mind obscure the Spirit in us. This is the total eclipse of a soul or our spiritual death. Life is (in) the Spirit, whereas death is in the realm of form.

◊

The Spirit Is Truth

Truth is often not the popular option, but truth is always the right way. Like a fish that swims upstream to meet its destiny, so should we strive to live an honest life despite being in the world of lies.

Truth sets us free from the bondage of lies. A lifetime of lies is nulled by one truthful confession.

Truth is a form of positive surrender.

Truth does not need to build an elaborate web of support to sustain its weight. Truth stands on its own.

Truth is wholesome and complete in itself.

Truth does not need us, but rather we need truth to continue to walk in the Spirit.

Truth is a form of worship to God. Those who lie quench the Spirit.

Truth is power.

◊

Walking in love and standing for truth do not

necessarily mean that we suffer or face the life of hardship. We can have good time in helping others. When we enjoy doing good then that is the worship of God in a real sense. When we have joy walking in the Spirit, God rejoices with us. We cannot find joy in worldly objects or from other people. The sense of happiness that we get from the world is short lived and addicting, whereas joy in the Spirit is like *"bubbling water out of a pool which keeps the water moving ."* A soul longs for joy, but often we seek it in the wrong places. Joy is within us, but we seek it in the world.

When we are spiritually aware, our thinking perspective shifts towards the spiritual light of selflessness. We are attracted by things that are virtuous and beneficial to everyone. Selfishness is the inherent nature of the flesh. Things that appeal to the flesh lose their luster to us when we are awakened in the Spirit, and ordinary things that we otherwise take for granted become vibrant. The world seen through an unfiltered vision appears encumbered with the barbwire of desires and temptations whose fruit are fear, guilt, shame, etc. We need to guard the mind each moment because the mind left on its own gravitates towards the spiritual darkness. A person who yields to the Spirit has lowered the barrier of the mind, and the mind is aligned with the Spirit. When the mind is under the Spirit, the soul abides in love, joy, peace, and freedom.

◊

Surrendering, Love, & Addictions

Surrender does not mean inaction, or lack of action on our part. Rather we let the Spirit guide us in doing what is the will of God. One strike squarely on the head of a nail is more effective than hundred strikes otherwise. Like a man trapped in a quicksand who struggles frantically only to sink deeper, we waste our opportunities, time, and other resources when we try to overcome a problem created by the carnal mind with the carnal mind. For example, a person trying to overcome an addiction cannot expect a lasting positive result by relying on the mind because all addictions are the mind made up. Our best effort will fail us and that will push us further into discouragement, frustration, and despair. The carnal mind will not readily give up its stronghold over us, much like a lion will give up his turf without a fierce fight. That is why we need power greater than the mind to overcome it.

If we are struggling with an addiction then we need to first acknowledge our helplessness in the carnal mind. *The carnal mind is not us*. We need to shed the light of Consciousness over the darkness of the carnal mind if we want to remove the darkness of addiction. We can ask God in prayerfulness to help us in overcoming an addiction by strengthening us against all temptations, and by bringing people or resources in our life which will be of help to us. We need to set our mind on things which will encourage us to stay on the path free from the addiction. In other words, the mind needs to be humbled before God for it to free its rein on us.

We should not treat an addiction as an enemy or a scourge. Doing so brings about negative judgment in us, even though the mind is under its control. Such judgment only alienates our positive attempts. We need to accept a weakness in the flesh with compassion for oneself. *"It is okay, no one is perfect in the flesh, and none can be."* As we let love spread in our heart, instead of fighting the addiction like a bitter enemy, we tame an addiction to finally overcome it. When a wild man named Angulimala once encountered Siddhartha Gautama (the Buddha), he wanted to kill Siddhartha Gautama so that he could add His finger on the garland of fingers he was wearing. The name Angulimala in Pali translates to a garland of fingers. Angulimala was in an evil mission in killing people he met and taking a finger from his victims as a souvenir, which he would wear around his neck. When he met Siddhartha Gautama, he did not see fear, hatred, or any kind of negative judgment in Him. The Buddha treated him with love and non-judgment. That encounter with Siddhartha Gautama transformed Angulimala to renounce all evil and become His disciple. The giants that we face in our daily life are not the physical beings like Angulimala, but they can be equally destructive. However, what the Buddha showed is still effective to us today. With love of the Spirit onto ourselves, we can overcome the giants of the mind.

Welcome love in your heart to surrender the fruits of the flesh to God.

◊

Humility is not humiliation, even though to the world it is synonymous to defeat and helplessness. When we are humble, we do not have the egoic need or burden to support our perception onto ourselves or others. When we are comfortable being in our skin, we do not constantly check our face in a mirror. When we take the lowest seat at a feast, we do not have to worry about being asked to take a lower seat. Social status, fame, money, education, physical stature, or sensual beauty is of and for the mind, and beyond the mind there is no attribute that separates us from the rest. The Spirit, which gives us our true identity, is One. As we become mature in the Spirit, we are attracted to the simple beauty that is everywhere, in everything and everyone. This is the beauty of being, of life, of creation, and of God; humility reveals that true beauty in us.

Humility is the acceptance of our being nothing to the world. But for the carnal mind to accept humility is synonymous to death. *Yet in dying of the ego is being alive in the Spirit.* Until the ego is buried in the dirt of worthlessness, the glory of the Self cannot be risen in us. This is the true resurrection of our soul. Two kings cannot rule a kingdom; one king needs to give up his power. When the sense of "I" is taken back from the ego and the soul identifies with the Spirit, we become like a strong, secure, and prosperous kingdom.

This is Enlightenment.

Vanity

The world can add thousands of praises onto us.

The world can shower us with all the riches.

The world can offer all kinds of the comforts and entertainment.

But what do all the praises, wealth, and comfort benefit a soul?

The body is reduced to dust, and we leave all behind.

Then all the time spent in the vain grasping profits nothing.

Each moment in life so precious, yet without the spiritual awareness we are all asleep.

Pride and greed quench the life out of life.

If you have the humility to let someone win a heated argument, it is not your weakness or pity for the other person, but rather your realization that prideful arguments only lead to dissent and destruction. People even lose their life because they are carried away by the ego for a brief moment of time. Dueling is one such example from the past, and the tendency in us is not dead. Notions like "Die in honor," "Men do not cry," etc.

are egoic pride, and it precludes us from saying "I am sorry" when we make a mistake. Inwardly we feel bad for our mistake, but we cannot stand up to take the responsibility for our wrong. If we ask ourselves what we gained by yielding to inhibition or pride, we realize that we did not really gain anything, except save the sense of being "somebody." But pride is not real or ours, because it is the inflated image of the ego. It is like a little cat that walks by candlelight and sees a lion in its shadow on a wall. What good is pride if it keeps our soul in this worldly bondage? Our soul longs for the freedom in the Spirit, but the ego is the impostor which robs us of our true home.

◊

Even when we go through sufferings in life, the carnal mind has the tendency to seek pity, and it secretly enjoys the attention like a little child. We have to be careful of this because as long as the mind is in control, we will not see the light within us. The gloomy cloud of ego will resist any positive change towards the bright day in the Spirit, and thus the ego keeps us in the cycle of ignorance and suffering. Surrendering to God is giving up of the secret pleasure of the carnal mind under suffering. Whereupon, there is no sense in thoughts such as, "Oh, sorry me!"

When we surrender our false identity to God, we accept what happened in our life in the past as the providence, and we aspire to be in God's favor, so to speak, for things yet to manifest by walking in love and truth. We do not regret for the past mistakes because we see ourselves helpless in the flesh then. This also brings about compassion in us for others. When we have gone through the bitter trials and tribulations in life, it is easier for us to relate ourselves to others who have fallen or been condemned by the society. We realize how the carnal mind is the prison for much of the population on earth, and that realization encourages us to love everyone regardless and pray for all.

◊

It would have been easy if we never had to face life's curve balls, or those excruciatingly painful phases in life. The reality is that everyone is vulnerable to the trials and tribulations in life, no matter how rich they are, how famous or successful they are, or even how wise or strong they are. If it were not so then there would not be the need for God or humility; we would all be like kings and queens parading pompously in our inflated world of vanity. The interesting thing, however, is that we are "Your Highness" in our own perception, though we may not want to acknowledge that. But in order to overcome the grip of the ego or the mind identity, we need to let go of the "good" feeling that comes from the attention that we get from others. That "good" feeling is very addictive; the more we have of it, the dire is the need to sustain it. Just look at the world of celebrity where famous people do anything to keep their fame. Some people even hurt themselves or put the lives of their loved ones in danger in order to get attention from others.

When we feel helpless on our own or when other people cannot or will not help us, then that's when we usually reach out to God. It is the feeling of vulnerability, like that of a little chick exposed to the elements soon after it is hatched, that we sense the need of a loving refuge. It is not necessarily that we get the physical refuge under a warm embrace like that of a loving hen, but the warm intuition of love in our heart is empowering none the less. No matter where we are in life we can feel that love of God because the Spirit of God is within us. The love of God brings us joy, and it is the source of peace which the world cannot give nor take away from us.

◊

Beside pride which is the polar opposite of humility, which is necessary in order to surrender our personal will onto God, we need to acknowledge other factors that keep us away from the grace of God. One such factors is our pleasure source. The sad part is that for many of us it is not comfortable surrendering our lives to God when it entails our giving up of our pleasure identity. Pleasure identity is that part of us which we know is not right but we continue to do so regardless. The pleasure source is derived from giving overtly into the fleshly desires. It can be overeating, drinking, debauchery, gossip, shopping, watching too much TV, gambling, etc.

To surrender to God is to derive our soul identity from the Spirit of God. We do not lose our identity to God. In fact, we give up something that is illusory (the ego) to attain what is real and eternal (perfection of our soul).

"Apart from God, whom or what can we surrender our life onto?"

Shall we surrender our life onto the government?

Well certainly no government is perfect from what we see the state of the countries in the world, and from the millions of people dead in countries like Stalin's Russia and Maoist China. [1,2]

Perhaps we can surrender our life onto the modern technology?

The technology is always evolving, and our surrender will need our constant updates!

What about our employer?

Our employment is not guaranteed, and when it ends, what shall we do? Update "God" in our resume?

The world and everything it represents is constantly changing and it is unreliable in the absolute term. We need something that is perfect, stable, powerful beyond the human might, and lasting beyond ourselves or the world to base our faith upon. If we go around the world searching for that something which encompasses all of these qualities, we will not be able to find one. This is because everything in nature changes and everything that humans make breaks or needs an upgrade. Only God is eternal and unchanging; only God is Almighty. Yet we cannot see God with the physical eyes, feel God with our hands, hear God with our ears, or experience God with our senses. God is beyond the mind and its senses, and to have faith in God we need to move beyond the mind.

People, while they are strong, can deny God all they want because they can "live" without needing any help from God. However, when people fall into grave circumstances, get old and weak, or the fear of death starts to tremble their heart, then they feel the need of God. Yet even being able to hear the soul calling in dire circumstances is through the grace of God because many will not be able hear a soul call amid pride and the noise of the world. Apart from God all things are vanity, even we, as this body or the mind, are vanity.

◊

It is relatively easier to surrender ourselves onto God when life's hardship takes its toll on us, and we can be assured that life will not always be easy. Thorns are part of a rose plant. However, surrendering ourselves to God is not as easy as one may think. We can say that we surrender to God all day long, but unless that utter humility dawns in on us, we are not able to transcend the threshold of the mind to step into the spiritual embrace. When the carnal mind is overcome, we experience freedom, and we have the peace of God. The sense of all pervasiveness, all-inclusiveness, all-divine automation reveals onto us through the Spirit. We can praise God and marvel, as we are a part of the whole and the whole is within us. That is also the beginning of the letting go of our impulsive hold on what is otherwise simply happening all along and all around. We do what is prompted to us through the Spirit, be it in a thought, intuition, sign, or suggestion or advice from other people. People who cross our path, things which we happen to see, hear, or a stranger who asks us for direction or just says "Hello," are all meant to be. All is happening accordingly in Godspace, and it is all divine automation. A soul moves along in Godspace according to its karma. There is no luck or coincidence in Godspace as God is omniscient. How can a ripple go unnoticed from the water in a pond?

Choices in life become evident when we are ready for them, otherwise it may as well have never existed for us. Depending on our karma, we are able to recognize the choices available to us and use our freewill to choose. Choices under the carnal mind are always limited because the carnal mind is biased and thus selective of what it thinks is right or good. We only need to look back in our past to realize the things that we could have done differently. Our choices are limited by the virtue of being in that particular point in our life. Our karma determines from the infinite number of paths that this present moment connects to. Perhaps it is for our own good that the future is obscured from us, otherwise the finite mind will be overburdened or overwhelmed than what it already is. Besides, life is an adventure, though bitter at times, yet rewarding to a soul when it eventually rests in the heavenly abode.

◊

The mind tries to control everything in life, whereas it does not even know when the last breath will occur for the body. The mind tries to grasp at everything that appeals to its senses. But all its best efforts will not avail anything if a certain thing is not meant for us. Though, if we try, we may get what we desire, but then we will have paid far more resources to get it. Besides, if a thing is not meant for us it will soon lose its appeal to the mind. Life is full of dents left by our unfulfilled desires, and yet had we got those things, we would have abandoned them like a child neglecting its barely used toy for a new one.

Watch your mind as it sees something beautiful, see how it tries to possess it, be it a new flat screen TV, new phone, or a beautiful woman or a handsome man. The answer is not giving into the mind's desires, but rather to overcome those urges. Overcoming the cravings of the mind is like cutting the root of a weed so that we do not have to deal with it again. When we surrender our desires and cravings to God, we let the power of the Spirit move us, and when we walk in the Spirit, we lack nothing because what we need is already provided for.

◊

Humility will open new doors in life for us, while pride will close open doors. Even those who may think that humility is a sign of weakness, yet they value humility inwardly. We just need to let the barrier of inhibition or pride of the carnal mind down in order to let the Spirit flow unrestricted. To say no to pride is an act of surrender. It takes inward strength to be attuned to the Spirit. So take every opportunity to walk in love, truth, to let go of pride, jealousy, greed, selfishness, callousness, and let your soul loose to fly in the vastness of Godspace.

Do not be afraid to appear a fool onto the world, nor be scared to appear weak before others. The feeling of freedom in the Spirit is worth every mocking and humiliation from the world. Those who have conquered their self have conquered the world. When you have overcome the carnal mind or the ego, the world loses its power to make you feel miserable. Then you are at peace, and you have joy in the Spirit. You are loved much more and in many ways than you think or acknowledge, and you are Love.

You are one with the One.

1 - http://necrometrics.com/20c5m.htm#Stalin

2 - http://necrometrics.com/20c5m.htm#Mao

Love Always Wins

There is an order amidst a confounding swarm of bees.
There is harmony amidst chaos in the multitude of people
in the world.
Love is the bond holding harmony and order.
Hearts rejoice and love always wins.

There is an oasis in the midst of a vast desert.
There is happiness after the agony of birth pang.
Love is the grace bringing happiness in an oasis.
Hearts intertwine and love always wins.

There is always a hope in our tribulations.
There is a certainty in thundering after a lightening.
Love is that power adding certainty to our hopes.
Hearts long for God and love always wins.

There is life in the movement of clouds.

There is beauty in the changing colors of the autumn leaves.
Love is that potion nurturing beauty in life.
Hearts seek for truth and love always wins.

There is joy in the revelation of the Spirit in a man.
There is a heavenly bliss in a soul enlightened.
Love is that blessing reaping the heavenly joy.
Hearts sing for God and love always wins.

Further Reading

The Buddha (Translated by Glenn Wallis)
> *The Dhammapada (Verses on the way)*

Thomas Nelson Publishers
> *New King James Version Bible*

Thomas
> *The Gospel Of Thomas*

Cardwells C. Nuckols
> *The Ego-Less SELF*, 2010

David R. Hawkings
> *Transcending The Levels of Consciousness*, 2006

David R. Hawkings
> *The Eye Of The I*, 2001

Lama Surya Das
> *Awakening The Buddha Within*, 1997

Eckhart Tolle
> *The Power Of NOW*, 1999

Glossary

Born again – Spiritual awakening in a person, or the opening of the third eye. This Christian term is comparable to Enlightenment in Buddhism.

Duality – The sense of separated- ness, like "I and you," "This and that." Duality is the realm of the mind. The mind is inherently selfish, incomplete, and it likes to compare and contrast everything.

Ego (The) – (The carnal mind or The flesh) The false sense of "I" which is the mind identity or form identity.

Enlightenment – Being aware of one's true identity in the Self, the Spirit of God, which comes about after transcending the false self of the mind identification.

Form – The physical realm of the world or creation, different from the spiritual realm. The mind is our interface to the realm of form.

Godspace – (Also the Consciousness or the Spirit) The Spirit of God which is all knowing, all encompassing, all powerful, and not bound by space or time (detail in Chapter 3).

Grace of God – Unconditional love of God as manifested in the creation. In Christian term, it is the unmerited favor shown freely by God as mercy onto the humanity for its redemption through the salvation in Christ.

Heart (spiritual) – The core of one's being, figuratively where our soul dwells. It is different from the physical heart, though often used synonymously.

I Am - Name of God as revealed in the Bible. However, there is no worldly name that can comprehensively define God because God is beyond the mind. God Is.

Mindfulness – The state of being aware of the present moment and the phenomena within and around us as they are happening.

Salvation – Saving of one's soul from the eternal damnation. This happens after one is born again (in the Spirit).

Samsara – A Buddhist word to denote this carnal world or a state full of pain and suffering.

Sangha – A Buddhist word in Sanskrit and Pali

languages used to denote a circle of practitioners with (generally) common belief and common interest in fellowship. Synonymous to a church.

self - The finite self, or the body or the mind identified entity. This word is used to represent a carnal man who is spiritually unawakened.

Self - The infinite Self, God, or the Spirit identified entity. This word is used to represent a soul which is spiritually awakened or Enlightened.

Soul – Identity or representation of us in the spiritual sense. There is the Spirit of God which is everywhere, and there is this "I" which can either identify with the Spirit or the mind. This "I" in a spiritual sense is a soul. Karma or heavenly treasure is associated with a soul. A soul is more local to us in a sense, while the Spirit is omnipresent.

Spirit (The) – (The Holy Spirit, Godspace, the Consciousness) God in the realm of the creation which is all inclusive, governing, maintaining, supporting, the Unmanifested, source of all manifest, yet undefinable, and unknowable with the mind. The Spirit gives us our true identity, and is the source of love, joy, and peace.

Subjective - Pertaining to one's personal experience or internalization as opposed to hearing, reading, or interpretation about something. For example, meditation is subjective, while reading or hearing about meditation is objective.

About The Author

Ramas Dev was born in Nepal, and has a cultural background in Buddhism and Hinduism from there. After coming to the United States, he was introduced to Christianity. His calling came in his early 30s. Life's trials and tribulations pushed him to seek further, and which brought about the spiritual awakening in him.

Mr. Dev has a degree in Computer Engineering. He enjoys outdoors and being close to nature. He likes listening to classical music and writing, among other things. He speaks in four languages and writes in two scripts. He also spends time helping others through local volunteering groups.

Mr. Dev can be reached via email at

ramasdev@mail.com

I Am HIS

To the world I am despised, to the Lord I am beloved
I have fallen, then I was raised

To the world I am worthless, to the Lord I am priceless
I lost all I had, then I won myself

To the world I am judged, in the lord I am free
I am condemned by the world, I am exalted in the Lord

To the world I am just as dead, to the lord I am alive
I died to the world, then I became alive in the Spirit of
God

To the world I am a burden, to the Lord I am His
I am estranged from the world, I am close to the Lord

To the world I am defiled, to the Lord I am sanctified
I became a worm to the world, then I was made a
butterfly

To the world I am helpless, in the Lord I am strong
I went through utter helplessness, then I was able to
have faith in God

To the world I am a fool, in the Lord I am wise
I became a laughter to the world, then I knew my worth
in the Lord

To the world I am an outcast, to the Lord I am dear
I went through hell, then I realized the heaven within

To the world I am a stranger, to the Lord I am His
beloved son
I am nothing to the world, I am everything in the Lord.

Thank You God
All glory belongs to You

Ω

www.ingramcontent.com/pod-product-compliance
Lightning Source LLC
LaVergne TN
LVHW051228080426
835513LV00016B/1469